ACTING
IS MY
DAY JOB

**7 STRATEGIES TO MARKET AND
MAKE MONEY AS AN ACTOR**

MATTHEW DEARING

"*Matt's a teacher who cares about the development of his students and who I trust to be honest and sincere in his direction. He's seen me through several artistic outlets and has been an encouraging creative coach for each.*"

—BRADLEY BAZILE, PRODUCER, DIRECTOR AND ACTOR

"*Matt wants nothing more than to serve others and make them into the best version of themselves. By teaching students to be better actors, he's making them better human beings. By becoming better human beings, they are in turn becoming better actors. Spending time with Matt in his studio, in his online classes or by reading his books will shape you and inspire you to be the best you that you can possibly be for those around you.*"

— ASHLEIGH PRICE, ACTRESS

"*Matt has such a unique way of teaching. He can always find a new way to push his students into the right direction in an absolutely loving way. Matt has taught me a lot not only about the art of acting but about my self, teaching me to stay confident in all of my choices and how to shape myself into the best person I can be. Matt has highly impacted my life in the best way possible.*"

—MICHAEL BROOKER, VOCALIST AND ACTOR

"*Knowing what's best isn't always easy to see for yourself. Matt has that uncanny ability to see through somebody, and really figure out what is best, and at the end, that's all that's left, the best.*"

—COLTON RODGERS, WRITER AND ACTOR

"*Matt's ability to intelligently and succinctly communicate with his students is unmatched. Not only is Matt a genuine individual he truly has his students best interests at heart.*"

—KEVIN WATHEY, ACTOR AND ENTREPRENEUR

"*I can disappoint myself, but I cannot disappoint him because he only wants to see his students succeed. Some of the people who impacted your life the most will never know. I hope he does. His character is shown by his genuine love. One of the most important lessons I have learned as an actor is how to be emotionally honest, this is what Matt Dearing teaches best.*"

—RACHEL SCHUMACHER, ACTRESS

"*Matt opened my eyes and made me realize that I don't have to be in LA to be a successful actor. I can make my own success and legacy wherever I happen to live.*"

—SERGEI LARSON, ACTOR

"*Matt has a wonderful balance of absolute authority over what he teaches, while maintaining a positive atmosphere focused on fun. Matt's impact on me has gone far beyond the bounds of acting. From our first interaction he welcomed me into a place where tools were sharpened, instruments tuned, and craft honed with passion, love, and mastery at the forefront of everything.*"

—JOSH LIND, ACTOR AND PROFESSIONAL DRIFTER

"The way Matt teaches is with love and genuineness. He teaches you to be honest and real, which correlates to life. Matt pushes you to the depths you want to but are too afraid to go. He has been a great inspiration in my growth as an actor and overall person. What can I say, I love this guy!"

—GABE JOHN, ACTOR AND POET

"Matthew Dearing has been a light and constant source of inspiration in my life. He has a servant's heart and at the same time is a visionary who searches for innovative ways to help others become the best versions of themselves. I would not be the man I am today without his guidance."

—BRIAN SWEENEY, INSPIRATIONAL SPEAKER AND ACTOR

"Matt's approach to coaching actors begins with creating the space for an actor to discover who she is. He encouraged me to accept who I am, my history, my personality, and my spirit, and to bring it into my work. Through that acceptance came the ability to grow and change as an individual. Matt has always encouraged me to experience life, and to use those experiences in my work. Without Matt's guidance, I would never have understood how to take the words in a script and fully embody them. Thank you, Matt for teaching me to lean into the parts of myself that scare me, to embrace my flaws, and to strive to become a better human and therefore, a better actor."

—RACHEL TAGGATZ, ACTRESS

"Matt is a kind and inspiring teacher. His dedication to the craft and knowledge of technique is a blessing to anyone lucky enough to work with him."

—MARLENE GALAN, ACTRESS

"Matt has challenged me to become a better version of myself, daily, and I know those lessons carry on through not only my acting and performing, but in life itself."

—JOHN LUKE GRUBB, ACTOR, DJ, DIRECTOR, PRODUCER

"Matthew Dearing has made it his life's mission to live, act, coach, learn, and love from truth. Not only is his passion so deeply fueled by his dream to create better human beings, but he gifts his students with so many invaluable skills that create true artists. He is changing the game of this industry and what it means to be a 'master' coach in the craft of Acting."

— SHEA ELYSSE TOEPEL, ACTRESS, CASTING COORDINATOR

"The only thing I can say is he doesn't treat me like I'm in a wheelchair. He treats me like an actor trying to get better! And pushes me not to settle!"

—KRISTINA KNOWLES, ACTRESS

"Matt has changed the way I listen and through personal development has changed the way I work and act."

—JOEY SWEENEY, ACTOR AND PROFESSIONAL VIDEO EDITOR

"He is patient and driven all at once. And humble."

—KARA PAULUS, ACTRESS

"Matt is insightfully genius, always bringing out the best possible performance from the actors he works with."

—SUSAN MATTHEW, ACTRESS

"I've worked with Matt Dearing on multiple projects via his studio. Having made multiple highly viral videos, he understands audiences and what they want to experience. He has incredible vision with the ability and drive to bring those visions to fruition. He cares about the quality of everything he's involved with, always striving for everyone around him to reach for and go beyond their fullest capabilities."

—TERRY CALIENDO, PRODUCER

"Matt Dearing and his studio have been a huge part in my growth personally and professionally. Matt teaches continuously about self acceptance. This is essential to becoming a truthful actor. It is a tremendous blessing to be able to study the craft of acting with him."

—ASHLEY HAMILTON, ACTRESS

"Matt has a way of breaking down the areas in need of improvement while simultaneously building the actor up. He reminds his students that there is no end point in the art of acting- it's a continuous, never-ending process and thus we as actors must find joy in the constant grind of improvement instead of focusing on crossing out x,y, and z on the to-do list we've created for ourselves that we believe must be completed before we can be considered a successful actor."

—JADA WARNER, ACTRESS

"Matt Dearing is a student of life. He pays attention to everything down to the smallest details and incorporates the little things into his teaching. He reminds us that every moment in the scene should be that way; moment to moment."

—GREG RENFRO, ACTOR

"Matt Dearing has the ability to articulate, challenge and direct that has catapulted me into new ways of thinking. He is constantly challenging me as an actor. I watch and listen to his direction and it causes me to turn down a new path which then leads me to another fork in the road and so on. It's a spiral effect that has opened my eyes and my mind to so many new learnings -a true light bulb moment happens over and over again."

— JENNIFER DIAMOND, ACTRESS

"Dearing Studio is easily one of the best schools I've attended - not just for acting but for life. Matt Dearing and the rest of the staff constantly challenge us to face our fears, exercise our empathy, and stretch our imaginations in ways we never dared - while providing a safe, friendly, and highly supportive environment. Every actor should be lucky enough to be taught here!"

— MICHAEL JUNG, ACTOR

Printed in the United States of America.
First printing edition 2019.

ISBN: 978-1-7332755-0-7 (Paperback)
ISBN: 978-1-7332755-3-8 (Hardcover)
ISBN: 978-1-7332755-1-4 (Ebook - Adobe PDF)
ISBN: 978-1-7332755-2-1 (Ebook - Kindle)
ISBN: 978-1-7332755-4-5 (Audio)

Library of Congress Control Number: 2019909212

Written by Matthew Dearing
Cover design and layout by Shaina Nielson
Edited by Chantel Hamilton

Dedicated to my wife, Leeann.
We met as two dreamers in a play about dreams, and
every day since has been a dream come true.

A special thank you to God, Mom, Dad, Kelly, Kim,
Joe, Val, Jack, Rosalyn, Marian, and Finn—your love
and support have been a constant inspiration.

Finally, to Brian, Joey, Shea, JL, and the rest of
our team at Dearing Acting Studio (past, present
and future), and to the thousands of actors who have
trained with us over the years—I love you all and wish
for you abundant joy throughout your journey.

TABLE OF CONTENTS

INTRODUCTION

Have you heard the fairytale about the acting industry dragon? It's a good one. Once upon a time, there was The Biz. The Biz is a ferocious, two-headed beast, fangs dripping with shredded dreams, waiting to eat her next victim and his shiny new headshots. Only the most daring venture near her cave. Most are either eaten alive or humiliated for turning back. Only the elusive "one-in-a-million," that bravest knight with exquisite bone structure, could master the beast... and even he needs to "know somebody who knew somebody." Nobody lives happily ever after. The end.

Oh, you've heard it? Great. Now you can take that story, crumple all the pages, and light them on fire. It's all lies; it's a way for the cynics to dismiss your dreams, and for the fearful to make the barrier for entry so high that they never even dare to push themselves there. Yes, you will have to work hard and train relentlessly in order to be excellent. I challenge you to name one worthy pursuit in the world that doesn't require the same effort. But it is possible to achieve this dream of becoming a professional working actor. You can do it, and I can prove it.

INTRODUCTION

If you want to do this thing—if you really want to be a great actor who gets paid to do what you love—keep reading. I'm going to lay out seven strategies to market yourself and make money as an actor right away. The big checks are out there waiting for those willing to put in the work. My goal is to help you overcome the fear of the dragon by laying down a solid foundation from the beginning. This way, you will set yourself up to capitalize on some early successes and build momentum toward establishing a lasting career in acting. All you have to do in this moment is ask yourself if you are ready.

Note: You may be tempted to skip around when reading, I'm ok with that. Just understand that all the chapters work together in harmony, and that you'll be required to act on everything in this book consistently and simultaneously to experience maximum results.

ACTING IS MY DAY JOB

CHAPTER 1

GET OUT THERE

"The big lesson in life, baby, is never be scared of anyone or anything."
—*Frank Sinatra*

The good news is that you are reading this, which means you've already begun. In truth, no one can tell you exactly how to go from complete obscurity into "fame," whatever that means. It's not a prescriptive, orderly path. One thing I do know, however, is that you have no chance whatsoever without making a commitment to getting started. This chapter lays out a few simple steps you can take to overcome your fear.

1. Take an acting class
2. Go to a networking event
3. Sign up on a few national audition sites
   (List available on website)
4. Audition locally, for everything and anything

TAKE A CLASS

This step doesn't have to be hard. There are plenty of good acting schools out there, and with a little research, you can find one near you to get started. Eventually, you will want to work your way toward earning a spot with a master teacher, who will challenge you in ways others cannot, but starting there is not necessary. You must accept where you are in order to strive for where you will go.

The first step in finding a good acting school is to read the reviews. We can't be naive to industry scams, and former students will almost always expose the crooks. Read carefully to see if you can discover each school's values. If they are aiming to make you better, that's a good sign. If they are promising to make you famous, that's a bad sign. Trust your instincts: if the promise sounds too good to be true, it's probably a scam. Just like you can't *actually* achieve a chiseled stomach in just five minutes a day, there isn't a magic formula for becoming rich and famous as an actor overnight. Anyone making this claim is just out to take your money, and you'll be on your way to experiencing the pain of going through an acting scam. This will not only empty your wallet, but will also drain you emotionally and kill your momentum.

The good news is that for every scam, you'll find dozens of reputable acting schools that operate with the intention of helping you grow as an artist. Once you've chosen your school, proceed immediately to Step 2: Get out of the car! I've heard countless stories of actors who showed up to our studio for the first time and just sat in the parking lot during class because they didn't have the guts to give it a try. Don't do that to yourself. Sign up and walk through the door before you have a chance to think.

You may read this book and realize that pursuing an actual career in acting is too much for you. That's okay, too. That's more self-discovery you've just done. Whether acting is an exploration or a lifelong passion, there's absolutely no downside to working the acting muscle. At our studio, we train doctors, lawyers, CEOs, real estate professionals, sales associates, and everyone in between. Some eventually fall in love and leave their old jobs behind. Others simply use the skills from class to advance further in their respective fields. So the bottom line is this: if you are feeling the pull to be an actor, it's your responsibility to follow through and at least try it out. Push yourself out of the "comfortable" and into the realm of possibility.

I'll finish this section by reiterating what you already know deep down in your stomach to be true: to be great at anything, you must train consistently for the rest of your life. If we can wrap our minds around this concept and stop looking for a proverbial finish line to cross, the journey becomes the most significant part of your experience. Your discoveries happen on the journey, not just at point B. This will be either scary or liberating, depending on your point of view. Don't get bogged down thinking about the cost of 20 years of training at the best acting schools in the world. That would be like someone who dreamed of becoming a doctor focusing on the cost of medical school before getting the prerequisites out of the way. Instead, realize that most people out there will struggle to make this a lifelong commitment; therefore, you will gain an enormous edge over everyone else simply by refusing to stop growing and bettering yourself. Make this step simple and easy. Commit to one class that fits in with your life. Then begin your journey by showing up and getting out of the car.

*Note: If you are not a beginner and have been at this for a while, make sure the school you train at is challenging. As you grow in skill, find coaches who are able to stretch your instrument in new ways.

GO TO A NETWORKING EVENT

Networking as an actor is something you have to do whether you like it or not. Since you are your product, you must get out of the house in order to let the market know that the product exists. Industry networking events can be a double-edged sword, but when you're first starting out, there's an upside to attending—if you know what you're doing. It's wise to take any steps you can to establish connections, especially if you are new to the area or haven't signed with an agency yet. Love it or hate it... but you have to do it. To find these events in your area, ask your acting instructor or other actors from class. You can also look into getting involved with your local production and Screen Actors Guild associations.

To make the most efficient use of your time, let me start by bringing light to some of the negative aspects you are sure to encounter. In theory, networking should be enjoyable: a room full of creatives and dreamers sharing successes, failures, and new ideas. It should be cooperative, edifying, and fun. Sadly I've come to find these events a bit wearisome. They seem to attract the most puffed up and egotistical among us. I'm sure this will offend some people, but unfortunately, it's true. Please hear me, readers: these are not bad people. They're not trying to hurt anyone. Generally they're just misguided or trying too hard. It's easy to identify the type: they're usually (loudly) discussing their latest indie film and muscling the attention of the nearest casting director to secure future bookings.

As a beginner on the scene, if not informed, you will tend to fall into the trap of feeling like the new kid at school. You'll hug the perimeter, maybe talk to a few other actors hanging around the refreshments table. You haven't gained entry to the boisterous, credit-spouting, name-dropping clique, and you wonder if you're doing something wrong. Don't sweat, new kid. The indie film they are discussing was probably a student project at a local community college. (And you should do some of those when you're starting out, by the way.) Don't worry if these people don't invite you to the table. That's not why you're here.

But I did tell you to show up, didn't I? So why are you here? There are a few things you should do to make the most out of these situations. Firstly, make sure you are showing up representing your brand. (See Chapter 4—Brand Yourself for more on this.) Second, stay in control. You can't listen at a high level if you're drinking too much or talking endlessly about yourself. And make no mistake, your job here is to listen. That's why you're here. Your job is not to come in and sell yourself to anyone with a pulse. Think outside yourself. Listen intently to the other artists in your community, ask good questions, and provide value wherever you can. Should you walk up and introduce yourself to the casting director in attendance? Of course you should. Your goal, when it's time to speak, should be to make an impression, ask a few good questions, and move on. Beyond that, focus on being intently observant of the atmosphere around you. Who's there, and who isn't? Who shows up for ten minutes to say hello and then leaves? Take notice without passing judgment. Gather and share contact information when appropriate, be faithful to yourself, and by all means, say hello—even when it's scary.

Once you establish relationships with the people who can hire you in town, you'll have all the information needed to capitalize on these events. Follow up with a "thank you" or "nice to meet you" email wherever applicable. Do your part to establish relationships with those whom you're genuinely interested in collaborating with in the future. The human element and authentic connections are, thankfully, still a large part of casting recommendations and decision making. This is not a bad thing, so don't be afraid of it. Show up for yourself. Keep track of who you meet. Work the room as a professional, and then feel free to leave. Now, onward and upward.

SIGN UP ON A FEW NATIONAL AUDITION SITES

Audition sites are a great resource for new actors, provided you have a strategy in place before enrolling. There are several advantages to these websites, and until you don't need them anymore, I highly suggest participating. Refer to www.dearingstudio.com/actingismydayjob for a list of recommended national audition websites.

Before I discuss how to systematically use these websites as a positive and powerful tool, let me point out what these websites will not do for you. National audition sites will not make you rich and famous. Nor will they be a free path to success. These websites require an investment of time and money in order to see a return.

"But won't I get access to lots of auditions?"

You will. But not all auditions are created equal. For example, in the acting industry, when a producer is trying to attract attention to a project, they often hold a national casting for a role that may end up going to a name actor, anyway. These casting sessions are held around the world, attracting thousands of people to line up for a chance to be a star. Early on in my career, I auditioned for a role in the movie *The Assassination of Jesse James by the Coward Robert Ford*—you know, that little movie starring Brad Pitt. In the casting call, they were looking for "a Casey Affleck type." I was asked to audition three times as the search narrowed, and they told me I was in the top three nationally. It was terribly exciting for me as a young actor, until the correspondences suddenly stopped without warning, and I soon found out they had cast none other than the actual Casey Affleck. We affectionately refer to these national probes within our industry as "cattle calls." National audition websites host a variety of auditions. Some are the digital version of a cattle call. Some will be auditions better suited for you and your specific casting type.

Knowing this, I'm still encouraging you to sign up. Why? These casting sites truly are a strategic tool for success as an actor for a few reasons. To begin with, it's nice when you're starting out to see how much "work" exists in different local markets around the world. It's a good reminder that you don't have to become an A-list celebrity in order to make a living at this. Every day, there are hundreds of thousands of jobs for up-and-coming actors across the world. They won't make you rich, but they will enable you to earn a living doing what you love.

Another advantage to these sites is that you don't have to wait for anyone else (i.e., an agent) to tell you that you're good enough to start auditioning. Instead, with the click of a few buttons, you are able to submit to hundreds of castings each and every day. You can audition for as many as you'd like, usually without having to leave your living room.

This leads me to the final (and perhaps most important) reason to be on these sites early in the process, which is simply *to learn how to audition*. There's no substitute for learning by doing. These websites give you the chance to learn through repetition and failure, the two most important teachers you'll ever have. (Read more on mastery in Chapter 7—Be a Great Actor.) In order to grow, you need scripts to score, you need to make choices about characters, and you need the pressure of an audition. There's no better way to get unlimited access to audition material. Worst-case scenario: you'll end up a better actor. Best case: you'll land a role. There's no downside to these sites unless you sign up without taking action. Think of this process like you would any other job search. If you are out of work, it's best to keep applying for jobs while you wait to hear back from the last interview. I'll admit that it stung a bit when Casey Affleck got that role, but let's be honest, he is absolutely more "the Casey Affleck type" than I am. In the end, I am grateful for the lessons learned through that experience. I believe the process of auditioning made me better, the failure to win the role made me stronger, and the reality check is something I can now share with others.

List of current National Audition Websites available at www.dearingstudio.com/actingismydayjob.

AUDITION LOCALLY, FOR EVERYTHING

When I say "get out there," I mean it. Don't give fear any room. It won't serve you. Take comfort in this: you are going to screw up, and that's how you learn. The mistake is the education. Add to this that nobody cares as much as you think they do. I've heard time and again to "wait until you're ready to begin auditioning because you don't want to make a bad first impression." But this logic is imperfect. Yes, you should have a little basic training under your belt before you see your first casting director in person. You should know what to do in an audition. But if you wait until you think you're "ready," you'll never go. Even an imperfect first impression is better than no impression. And if you make a bad impression, get better and come back again. Evaluate what missteps you made in the audition room, and ask yourself what you can do to grow and learn from each audition. (See Chapter 2—Get Organized for a comprehensive audition evaluation template.) You'll be noticed for your progress, not remembered by your last failure.

In the early years of my acting career, I was so hungry, I would do anything to get my face out there. I did things that were so idiotic I can't help but sit back and laugh. Here's an example of what not to do because it doesn't work. My first attempt at marketing myself included a cropped photo of me at a party with beer bottles in the background. (Forehead slap.) I broke every single rule. The picture wasn't in focus. I printed it on cheap photo paper at my house. When I got myself out there to take my first class, it was with a local casting director who called me up in front of the room to discuss publicly why my picture was the worst headshot she had seen in twenty years of casting. To make matters worse, one week earlier, I had gone to every major college and local trade school to hang posters with this dazzling headshot (along with pull-off tabs containing my phone number), offering my services as an actor. Yeah, I really did that. And no, I didn't get a single phone call.

Was this idea crazy and completely absurd? Undoubtedly. Did I show off how desperate and clueless I was? Without question. On the other hand, I'm proud of that naive kid who was hungry enough to put himself out there. Though this move was moronic—and I repeat, *do not hang your picture around town*—at least I was taking action. I was willing to think outside the box and fail big time in order to get better. It will take exactly this type of tenacity to be successful as an actor. I can tell you this story ends with that same casting director retiring three years later, but not before booking me on two major local projects. I got knocked down hard in the first few years but continued to consistently learn the business and train like a madman. My first impression was a bad one, but I got better and she took notice of the progress.

There are jobs for actors of every shape, size, and skill level. Opportunities are available in every city around the world. But you have to get out there. You may have to turn over some rocks, but I promise you, there is someone nearby with a camera, working at becoming the next Spielberg. Go find that person, and grow together. Do it for free for as long as you have to. You work for free because when you start out, that is what you are worth. Then, from consistently working and training, you will gradually increase the value you bring to each project. You will earn the right to be discerning with your time and creative energy. As one of my favorite acting coaches, Larry Moss, loves to say, "Become so good that they *have* to hire you."

*Note: Remember this: your audition begins as soon as you pull into the parking lot. You never know what key players are observing you. This is not paranoia or over-preparation; this is playing the game, and you must present the best version of yourself as soon as you enter the atmosphere.

CHAPTER 2

GET ORGANIZED

"Do what you have to do, to do what you want to do."
—Denzel Washington

Working actors must navigate and manage several moving parts at the same time. You'll be juggling everything discussed in this book. The list includes, but is not limited to, acting classes, agents and managers, family, friends, auditions, social media, headshots, callbacks, money, actor website, memorization, travel, and marketing. A daunting list as it stands, and I've left out the bit about creating your own content, which I highly recommend. You'll read more about that in Chapter 5—Be a Producer, but for now, just understand that process comes with its own laundry list of things to remember.

Needless to say, organization can make or break you. Most actors figure this out down the line and struggle to catch up. I know, because I was one of those actors. This chapter explores the essential categories needed to create an Actor Notebook, stay organized, track progress, and be prepared when others are not. You'll discover all the tools needed to create a personalized system for actor success.

Feel free to customize your own process, notebook materials and tracking systems. It doesn't matter how you come by it. The important thing is to use it.

1. Create an actor notebook

    1.1 Accountability checklist

    1.2 Important information

    1.3 Current projects

    1.4 Auditions

    1.5 Expenses

    1.6 Goals

    1.7 Progress

    1.8 Inspiration

    1.9 Notes

2. Bonus: expect the unexpected

CREATE AN ACTOR NOTEBOOK

That's right, kids. Break out the Lisa Frank pencil case 'cause you're going to buy school supplies. You'll need a three-ring binder, dividers, label maker, paper, and a good system. If you're serious about taking your career to the next level, block off some time to implement this method of growing, tracking, and staying organized.

Below, I've shared a list of essentials and organizational examples. Customizable PDF downloads for each page described are available at www.DearingStudio.com/ActingIsMyDayJob. This system works, so use it. You may need to make alterations based on the market you are in, but the basics are the same no matter where you live.

1. One-inch three-ring binder with a slot for an interchangeable cover
2. Dividers with clear tabs
3. Label maker
4. Paper

THE BINDER

I like the one-inch version because it's big enough to hold a lot of information, but not so big that I'll be tempted to become a script hoarder. (That's a real thing.) This size notebook will require regular tending to remain organized. That's a good thing. You want to be interacting with your Actor Notebook often. It keeps your goals and metrics in front of you. It will help you visualize where you are going and hold you accountable for what you have and haven't done. Eventually, you'll need a small filing system (or a digital one) to keep track of your year for reference later, but go ahead and get through the first year before making that purchase.

The interchangeable cover is important because you need to be proud of and inspired by your notebook. I've changed my cover over the years to reflect specific lessons/obstacles I was working through, current inspiration, or what I wanted next.

Make sure the binder has pockets so you can store several headshots and resumes with you at all times. If your agent requires them, you can use the other pocket for talent vouchers. Then create dividers for each section found below and begin organizing your career.

*Note: A talent voucher is essentially a time card for actors to prove you arrived on set. This document will give your agent the ability to collect payment if necessary. Each agent will have their own personalized form and protocol for filling them out.

THE DIVIDERS

You'll need eight or more dividers. Here are the sections included in our system. A PDF download of each page is available at www.DearingStudio.com/ActingIsMyDayJob.

1. **Accountability checklist**

   This should be the first thing you see when opening your notebook. This section is a weekly to-do list that will be adjusted regularly. It's best to interact with it every day and be honest with yourself about whether your actions are getting you closer to your goals. For ease, we label this section CHECKLIST.

2. **Important information**

   There are things you need to know on the fly as an actor that most people don't think about. Having this section updated and easily accessible will make you look professional and will save your most precious resource: time. We provide two PDFs in our system. The first includes a space for you to fill out the following: agent/manager contact, local casting director contact, local Screen Actor's Guild (SAG) contact info, actor size sheet (with accurate body measurements for wardrobe), and anything else you may need to fill out or recall in a last-minute audition. The second is an ongoing list of producers and directors you have worked with or met at industry networking events. Once on a set, be sure to get the contact info of the person in charge. This will give you an opportunity to build a relationship after the gig is over, as well as the ability to track down the footage for your demo reel. (More on this in Chapter 4—Brand Yourself).

3. Current projects

This section is set aside for scripts, including any jobs you have been hired on or that you are workshopping in your acting class.

*Note: There should always be "something" in this section. To be a working actor, you must constantly be working on your next project, whether you're getting paid or not.

4. Sides & Auditions

You're going to love this section, friends. Think of it as the secret sauce needed to progress as fast as possible into making money as an actor. Here you will keep the "sides" (sections of a script used for auditioning purposes) for current/ upcoming auditions you are preparing for. Once the audition is complete, remove the sides from this section and throw away or file for future practice. It is then important to track every audition and callback so that you have a record of how you prepared, your own feeling of your performance, areas of improvement for next time, and the results that followed. Be sure to fill out how you felt about your performance right after you audition and how you could have improved (and there's always room for improvement, no matter how great you did). You may be surprised when you reflect on your auditions. Perhaps the one you thought went poorly resulted in a callback or booking, or vice versa. At our studio, we refer to this as learning from your "game tape." Much like an athlete would evaluate their performance on the field after each game, you will be able to observe your actions objectively with the intent to improve no matter what the outcome. You must be honest about the work in order to hold yourself accountable. The only way to run metrics on your audition success is to faithfully record them, each and every time.

5. Expenses

We'll talk more specifically about the fact that you are essentially running your own small business in Chapter 6— Run the Business. So without going into too much detail, just know that this section is where you'll make money by saving money. As a business owner, you are entitled to a few benefits that go along with starting a company and contributing to the economy. Many of your expenses are considered tax write-offs, including acting classes (both online and studio), travel, car, gas, advertising, agent commissions, office supplies, business meals, cell phone, internet, union dues, and props. Even going to the movies can be a write-off if tracked properly! You'll need to research tax codes as they change frequently, and you'll also need the help of a good accountant to ensure everything is above board. Like any start-up business, your first few years might see you operating in the red, and that's OK. Just be smart enough to become informed so that you're not throwing money away!

6. Goals

You have to decide on a destination before you plot a course. Goals are enormously important; you probably already know that if you're reading this book. You can find helpful goal-setting worksheets all over the internet, and we've included a template for you at www.DearingStudio.com/ ActingIsMyDayJob. While we won't have time to delve into the nitty-gritty of goal setting, we've created some guidelines to get you going. (If you need more help in this area, there is an entire dissertation specifically geared toward actor goals that can be found within the Dearing Acting Studio e-course "Be a Great Actor No Matter Where you Live.") which can be found at www.DearingStudio.com

For now, I will summarize the philosophy in one sentence: dream big for ten years from now, then narrow down to the smallest daily achievement that can be accomplished today to get you one step closer to that dream. Think about where you want to be in ten years. Good. Now where would you need to be in five years to make that realistic? In one year? In six months? In one month? In a week? You see what I'm doing here. Your small, daily choices have to support your big picture dreams. I suggest making this section a high priority. Once you identify where you want to end up, you will feel motivated to complete all the other categories in your actor notebook! Starting with goals provides beautiful scaffolding for the discipline of the daily grind that lies ahead.

7. Progress

You need this section so you don't end up in the loony bin pulling your hair out because you feel like nothing is happening. If you have the passion to follow the instructions in this book, progress is inevitable. Most people don't come close to making a living at this simply because they get discouraged and give up. In this section, you will keep a journal of all the positive steps you've taken thus far. Trust me that without it, you'll end up feeling like you're watching the grass grow in the front yard. Taking inventory of what you have done will enable you to reflect on the progress you've made when the self-doubt inevitably creeps up on you. You can squash that insecurity with a healthy dose of remembering that "just four months ago, I was terrified to step into my first acting class, and now I've memorized three monologues and gone out for two auditions." Tracking your progress will allow you celebrate the small wins along the way and remember that life is all about the journey.

8. Inspiration

To be the best, you need a winning mindset. This one-page sheet should be updated every month with a personal affirmation and three quotes from actors who have already gone where you plan to go.

9. Notes

This is a section for acting class notes. Be prepared as you walk into an acting class. Expect to learn a plethora of new things that you'll definitely wish you brought a pen and paper to class for. Need I say more?

10. BONUS: Character Breakdown Worksheet

Use this worksheet to develop every character you play. Keep these somewhere so you can look back at all the characters you've created over your lifetime as an actor.

ACCOUNTABILITY CHART

Print a copy for every area of accountability.
Examples: Training, Marketing, Finances, Content Creation, etc.

DAY/MONTH/YEAR:

AREA OF ACCOUNTABILITY

Training

ONGOING RESPONSIBILITIES

1. Excercise
2.
3.
4.
5.
6.
7.
8.

CURRENT TO-DO LIST

1. Acting Class
2. Research new vocal warmup
3. HIRE Personal trainer
4.
5.
6.
7.
8.
9.
10.
11.
12.

NOTES

I'm feeling as if I'll never truly make it in the acting industry. I feel I'm not skinny, or pretty enough or if I even have the talent people are looking for but all I can do is work, wish, try and hope for it.

ACCOUNTABILITY CHART

Print a copy for every area of accountability.
Examples: Training, Marketing, Finances, Content Creation, etc.

DAY/MONTH/YEAR: *10/14/18*

AREA OF ACCOUNTABILITY

Training

ONGOING RESPONSIBILITIES

1. *Acting class*
2. *Voice*
3. *Diction*
4. *Movement*
5. *Exercise*
6.
7.
8.

CURRENT TO-DO LIST

1. *Memorize scene for class*
2. *Buy cork for new diction exercise*
3. *Research new vocal warm-up*
4. *Sign up for a dance class*
5. *Hire personal trainer*
6. *Meet with scene partner*
7. *Finish my character background work*
8. *Practice cold reads*
9.
10.
11.
12.

NOTES

I'm feeling good from all the hard work last week.
Starting to feel some momentum. Had a rough audition on Wednesday but class that night was
amazing. Gotta keep eating right and stay focused, as I know I'm on the right path!

IMPORTANT INFO

REFERENCE SHEET

AGENT INFO:

Agent Name:
Office Number:
Cell Number:
Email: FIP710005@ gmail.com
Address:
Website:
Agency Contact:

ACTOR SIZING INFO					
height	dress	shirt	shoe	hair *blonde*	
waist	suit	pant	neck	eyes *brown*	

Casting Director:

Office address:

Phone number:

Casting Director:

Office address:

Phone number:

Casting Director:

Office address:

Phone number:

IMPORTANT INFO

REFERENCE SHEET

AGENT INFO:

Agent Name: *Agency Owner Name*
Office Number: *(555) 123-4567*
Cell Number: *(555) 123-4567 (Agent Cell if you have it)*
Email: *Agent booking email*
Address: *Agency Office Address*
Website: *Agentwebsite.com*
Agency Contact: *Agency Direct Contact*

ACTOR SIZING INFO				
height *inches/feet*	dress *6*	shirt *m/l*	shoe *8.5*	hair *blonde*
waist *inches*	suit *40 reg*	pant *waist x inseam*	neck *circumference*	eyes *brown*

Casting Director: *Name*

Office address: *Company. 12345 N. 1st St. Denver, CO*

Phone number: *(123) 123-4567*

Casting Director:

Office address:

Phone number:

Casting Director:

Office address:

Phone number:

CONNECTIONS AND CONTACTS

PRODUCERS / DIRECTORS / INDUSTRY
Use this space as a contact info reference sheet for people you have met while networking or have worked with on various projects.

PROJECT / EVENT   ACTOR'S ROLE (*IF APPLICABLE)

Project/Event:

Date:

Notes:

Character Name:

Role Type:

Character's purpose to project/event:

PROJECT / EVENT CONTACTS:
- Fill this space with contact info of agents, crew members, fellow actors, coaches, etc.

Name:
Company/Title:
Phone:
Email:

Name:
Company/Title:
Phone:
Email:

Name:
Company/Title:
Phone:
Email:

Name:
Company/Title:
Phone:
Email:

Name:
Company/Title:
Phone:
Email:

Name:
Company/Title:
Phone:
Email:

"Actors, you know, they're often awkward people in real life." –Liev Schreiber

CONNECTIONS AND CONTACTS

PRODUCERS / DIRECTORS / INDUSTRY
Use this space as a contact info reference sheet for people you have met while networking or have worked with on various projects.

PROJECT / EVENT   ## ACTOR'S ROLE (*IF APPLICABLE)

Project/Event: *Desert and Sun Patio Commercial Shoot*

Date: *11/22/18*

Notes: *Shoot was fun. I was a little nervous upon arrival but once I settled in everything was great. Director was impressed with my preparation!*

Character Name: *Katie*

Role Type: *Principle*

Character's purpose to project/event: *Interact with sales associate while shopping for a spa*

PROJECT / EVENT CONTACTS:
- Fill this space with contact info of agents, crew members, fellow actors, coaches, etc.

Name: *Ryan Smith*
Company/Title: *Producer*
Phone: *(555) 123-4567*
Email: *email@email.com*

Name:
Company/Title:
Phone:
Email:

Name: *Candice Meyer*
Company/Title: *Assistant Director*
Phone: *(555) 123-4567*
Email: *email@email.com*

Name:
Company/Title:
Phone:
Email:

Name:
Company/Title:
Phone:
Email:

Name:
Company/Title:
Phone:
Email:

"Actors, you know, they're often awkward people in real life." –Liev Schreiber

ACTOR AUDITION TRACKER

DATE: _____
☐ **AUDITION**   ☐ **CALLBACK**
PROJECT: _____
ROLE: _____
CASTING DIRECTOR: _____

NOTES:
1. How much time was given between audition notice and audition? How much time was spent preparing for your audition?

_____
_____
_____

2. What important information can be extracted from the audition notice? (Wardrobe, style, feel, sides, director, etc.)

_____
_____

3. Describe your process as you prepared for your audition. What feelings did you bring into the audition with you?

_____
_____

4. Were there any specific elements of your audition that surprised you? (Direction, set up, technical difficulty, etc.)

_____
_____
_____

5. How would you rate your performance? What would you change about your audition preparation for the future?

_____
_____
_____

☐ **BOOKED**   ☐ **CALLBACK**   ☐ **NOTHING**

"If it wasn't hard, everyone would do it. It's the hard that makes it great." –Tom Hanks

ACTOR AUDITION TRACKER

DATE: _____
☑ **AUDITION** ☐ **CALLBACK**
PROJECT: _Desert and Sun Patio_
ROLE: _Customer_
CASTING DIRECTOR: _Sean Smith_

NOTES:

1. How much time was given between audition notice and audition? How much time was spent preparing for your audition?
The script was sent out 4 days before the audition took place. I spent around 2 hours each day rehearsing.

2. What important information can be extracted from the audition notice? (Wardrobe, style, feel, sides, director, etc.)
The wardrobe was casual, fun, so I felt confident that I could be myself. It seemed as though they were looking for high energy, "real" people, improvisational experience and comedic training.

3. Describe your process as you prepared for your audition. What feelings did you bring into the audition with you?
I memorized the lines monotone and without voice inflection to make sure I had the lines committed to memory, then I tried different physicality's, voices and perspectives for each role to see what felt most natural. Overall, I was excited for the audition. I felt confident and ready.

4. Were there any specific elements of your audition that surprised you? (Direction, set up, technical difficulty, etc.)
The client was actually in the room for the audition which is nerve-racking, but as soon as I signed in and was assigned my audition partner, we practiced a few times, built a connection and did our best.

5. How would you rate your performance? What would you change about your audition preparation for the future?
I was happy with my performance, although there is already room for growth. I would give myself a 7 out of 10. I would change my focus with my next audition and ensure that there are no distractions around while I memorize and rehearse.

☐ **BOOKED** ☑ **CALLBACK** ☐ **NOTHING**

"If it wasn't hard, everyone would do it. It's the hard that makes it great." -Tom Hanks

ACTOR EXPENSE SHEET

MONTH/YEAR:

	ACTING CLASSES	TRAVEL	MILEAGE	ADVERTISING	AGENT/ UNION FEE	BUSINESS MEALS	ULTILITY BILLS	OFFICE SUPPLIES	PROPS/ COSTUME
	ONLINE, STUDIO, WORKSHOPS, ETC	GAS, AUTO MAINTENCE, ETC	MILAGE TO AND FROM CLASSES, AUDITIONS, BOOKINGS, ETC	HEADSHOTS, DEMO REEL, CLIENT GIFTS, BUSINESS CARDS, WEBSITE FEES, ETC	AGENT PERCENTAGE OF BOOKINGS, SAG-SAG AFTRA, ETC DUES	MEALS PURCHASED WHEN ON AN AUDITION, CALLBACK, BOOKING, ETC	INTERNET, CABLE, CELL PHONE, MISCELLANEOUS BILLS	DUPPLICE FOR BRAND	MATERIALS, COSTUMES OR PROPS ACQUIRED FOR AUDITIONS, CALLBACKS, BOOKINGS, ETC
WEEK 1									
Monday									
Tuesday									
Wednesday									
Thursday									
Friday									
Saturday									
Sunday									
WEEK 2									
Monday									
Tuesday									
Wednesday									
Thursday									
Friday									
Saturday									
Sunday									
WEEK 3									
Monday									
Tuesday									
Wednesday									
Thursday									
Friday									
Saturday									
Sunday									
WEEK 4									
Monday									
Tuesday									
Wednesday									
Thursday									
Friday									
Saturday									
Sunday									
TOTALS									

Notes: _____

Income/Budget: _____

_____   _____
_____   _____
_____   _____
_____   _____
_____   _____
_____   _____
_____   _____

ACTOR EXPENSE SHEET

MONTH/YEAR: 01/2019

	ACTING CLASSES	TRAVEL	MILEAGE	ADVERTISING	AGENT/ UNION FEE	BUSINESS MEALS	ULTILITY BILLS	OFFICE SUPPLIES	PROPS/ COSTUME
	ONLINE, STUDIO, WORKSHOPS, ETC.	GAS, AUTO MAINTENCE, ETC.	MILAGE TO AND FROM CLASSES, AUDITIONS, BOOKINGS, ETC.	HEADSHOTS, DEMO REEL, CLIENT GIFTS, BUSINESS CARDS, WEBSITE FEES, ETC.	AGENT PERCENTAGE OF BOOKINGS AND SAG DUES (AFTRA), ETC. DUES	MEALS PURCHASED WHEN ON AN AUDITION, CALLBACK, BOOKING, ETC.	INTERNET, CABLE, CELL PHONE, MISCELLANEOUS BILLS	SUPPLIES FOR BRAND	MATERIALS, COSTUMES OR PROPS AQUIRED FOR BOOKINGS, CALLBACKS, BOOKINGS, ETC.
WEEK 1									
Monday	$150.00 (MONTHLY)	$40.00 (WEEKLY)	50 MILES	$75.00 ANNUAL WEBSITE RENEWAL	20% AGENT FEE FOR "X" SHOOT	$10.00	$200.00 (MONTHLY)	$75.00 (SOCIAL E-COURSE)	$100.00 (NEW AUDITION OUTFIT)
Tuesday			50 MILES			PACKED LUNCH			
Wednesday			50 MILES			PACKED LUNCH			
Thursday			50 MILES			$12.00			
Friday			50 MILES			$15.00			
Saturday	$75.00 WORKSHOP		50 MILES			HOME FOR MEALS			
Sunday			50 MILES			HOME FOR MEALS			
WEEK 2									
Monday		$40.00							
Tuesday									
Wednesday									
Thursday									
Friday									
Saturday									
Sunday									
WEEK 3									
Monday		$40.00							
Tuesday									
Wednesday									
Thursday									
Friday									
Saturday									
Sunday									
WEEK 4									
Monday		$40.00							
Tuesday									
Wednesday									
Thursday									
Friday									
Saturday									
Sunday									
TOTALS									

Notes: This was a great month for me! Starting to see some momentum and the power of goal setting. Crazy I landed three gigs that all paid this month. Time to make my goals bigger. As expected my expenses were higher this month due to more activity. So grateful for my acting classes and network that has been so supportive. I'm gonna give myself the win this month and celebrate this success by investing in new headshots and an additional acting class.

Income/Budget:

MONEY IN FROM ACTING - $500 (ON CAMERA HOST) / $250 (STUDENT FILM) / $2,500 (COMMERCIAL JOB)

TOTAL - $3,250.00

MONEY IN FROM OTHER JOBS - $450 (FREELANCE WRITING) / $1,250 (GOLF COURSE JOB) TOTAL - $1,700.00

BUDGETED EXPENSES TOTAL - $750

ACTUAL EXPENSES - $980

GOAL SETTING FOR ACTORS

Use this space to list out your goals for the year, then choose the most important of those goals to create monthly goals. Then, create weekly goals that will help set deadlines to reach your ultimate yearly goal. Repeat every month.

MONTH/YEAR:

MY ANNUAL GOALS (LIST 5 "BIG PICTURE" GOALS FOR YOUR YEAR)

1.

2.

3.

4.

5.

MY MONTHLY GOALS (LIST 5 MONTHLY GOALS THAT WILL HELP YOU REACH YOUR NUMBER ONE GOAL FOR THE YEAR.)

GOAL FOR YEAR:

1.

2.

3.

4.

5.

MY WEEKLY GOALS (LIST 3 GOALS YOU CAN ACCOMPLISH EACH WEEK TO OBTAIN YOUR NUMBER ONE GOAL FOR THE MONTH)

WEEK 1	WEEK 2	WEEK 3	WEEK 4
1	1	1	1
2	2	2	2
3	3	3	3

"A goal is not always meant to be reached, it often serves as something to aim at." –Bruce Lee

GOAL SETTING FOR ACTORS

Use this space to list out your goals for the year, then choose the most important of those goals to create monthly goals. Then, create weekly goals that will help set deadlines to reach your ultimate yearly goal. Repeat every month.

MONTH/YEAR: *February / 2018*

MY ANNUAL GOALS (LIST 5 "BIG PICTURE" GOALS FOR YOUR YEAR)

1. *Memorize fifteen monologues*
2. *Audition for fifty projects*
3. *Read twenty plays*
4. *Add twenty people to my contact sheet*
5. *Produce/direct a short film*

MY MONTHLY GOALS (LIST 5 MONTHLY GOALS THAT WILL HELP YOU REACH YOUR NUMBER ONE GOAL FOR THE YEAR.)

GOAL FOR YEAR: *Create a demo reel*

1. *Memorize new scenes/monologue*
2. *Audition for one project every month to refine skills*
3. *Take an acting workshop*
4. *Learn a new dialect/accent*
5. *Write research material for reel*

MY WEEKLY GOALS (LIST 3 GOALS YOU CAN ACCOMPLISH EACH WEEK TO OBTAIN YOUR NUMBER ONE GOAL FOR THE MONTH)

WEEK 1	WEEK 2	WEEK 3	WEEK 4
1 *find auditions*	1 *find auditions*	1 *find auditions*	1 *find auditions*
2 *audition 3 times*	2 *audition 3 times*	2 *audition 3 times*	2 *audition 3 times*
3 *track auditions*	3 *track auditions*	3 *track auditions*	3 *track auditions*

"A goal is not always meant to be reached, it often serves as something to aim at." –Bruce Lee

ACTOR PROGRESS SHEET

Use this space to journal specifics about your mindset this month.
Be honest and repeat every month.

MONTH/YEAR:

What, if any, obstacle or fear is holding me back right now?

It's currently 4.22.22 and my fear is I'll never be good enough to cut. Such as my body, face and talent and there is no stability in my life,

Is there anyone in my life who has been consistently negative? Describe:

Myself and my own thoughts

What is one obstacle or fear I am working on or have overcome?

Rejecting myself and not believing in myself

What is a personal discovery I recently made?

That I can act as hard as it is I have potential.

What is one new acting lesson I have learned?

Not to be afraid of rejection bcuz if one thing doesn't work out something else was meant to be.

What is one accomplishment I have achieved?

"Ease is a greater threat to progress than hardship" –Denzel Washington

ACTOR PROGRESS SHEET

Use this space to journal specifics about your mindset this month.
Be honest and repeat every month.

MONTH/YEAR: *06/2018*

What, if any, obstacle or fear is holding me back right now?
I am currently scared to audition for an agent for fear of rejection.

Is there anyone in my life who has been consistently negative? Describe:
My friend Bobby has been making negative remarks about my acting that throw me off. I will need to monitor this and either bring it up or move on from that friendship.

What is one obstacle or fear I am working on or have overcome?
I was terrified to take Improv class and this last month I just went for it. At first I was really shy but now after only a few weeks I'm really starting to love it.

What is a personal discovery I recently made?
This is crazy, but I discovered this last week that getting up just one hour earlier has made me exponentially more productive. Keep it up!

What is one new acting lesson I have learned?
I mentioned this above, but I've learned not to be afraid of Improv and also that Improv was not at all what I thought it was.

What is one accomplishment I have achieved?
I read a new play and memorized one shakespeare monologue. Feels really good.

"Ease is a greater threat to progress than hardship" –Denzel Washington

37

BE INSPIRED

PERSONAL AFFIRMATION:
Begin and end your day by repeating your personal affirmations. These must be in the present tense and include gratitude.

_____

_____

_____

_____

_____

_____

_____

_____

_____

_____

_____

_____

_____

_____

_____

_____

_____

INSPIRATIONAL ACTOR QUOTE:
Insert a quote from a performer you look up to that will remind you to continue to move your floor of success.

_____

_____

_____

BE INSPIRED

PERSONAL AFFIRMATION:
Begin and end your day by repeating your personal affirmations. These must be in the present tense and include gratitude.

I am so happy and grateful now that I have committed to becoming a better actor each and every day.

I am so happy and gratful now that I am pursuing my dreams

I am so happy and grateful now that I've committed to daily exercise in order to be the best version of myself as an actor

I am so happy and grateful now that I am organized as an actor

I am so happy and grateful now that I have developed the mindset to make Acting My Day Job!

INSPIRATIONAL ACTOR QUOTE:
Insert a quote from a performer you look up to that will remind you to continue to move your floor of success.

"Only you and you alone can change your situation." - Leonardo DiCaprio

CHARACTER BREAKDOWN

This series of questions is designed to generate ideas for your character's backstory, motivations, influences and circumstances. Answer questions from the character's perspective.

BASIC CHARACTER QUESTIONS:

1. What is your full name? (First, Middle, Last)
2. When were you born and what is your astrological sign?
3. Where did you grow up?
4. Where do you live now? (Be as specific as possible)
5. What was your childhood like?
6. Describe your relationship with your mother.
7. Describe your relationship with your father.
8. How do you make a living?

INDIVIDUALITY CHARACTER QUESTIONS:

9. What is your favorite color?
10. Do you have a favorite sport you enjoy watching?
11. What is your favorite activity to participate in?
12. What is your favorite television program?
13. What are your hobbies?
14. What type of music do you listen to?
15. List three of your favorite foods.
16. What is your Political Affiliation?
17. Do you have any addictions?
18. Do you have children? Do you like children?
19. What religion are you?
20. What type of house (apartment) do you live in?
21. Do you take drugs or have you ever?
22. Do you smoke or drink?
23. What newspapers do you read?
24. What was the last book you read?
25. Who's your favorite actor/actress?
26. How does your character dress?
27. Who in this world do you most admire?
28. What animal best represents who you are?
29. Describe your "happy place".

CHARACTER BREAKDOWN

PERSONALITY CHARACTER QUESTIONS:

30. What type of humor makes you laugh? (Think of two jokes your character would laugh at and tell them in character to someone.)
31. What is your strongest physical attribute (i.e. Face, Body...)?
32. What is it about your body that you like least?
33. What is your strongest attribute? (i.e. Honesty, Perceptiveness, Humor...)
34. What is your weakest personality trait? (i.e. Impatience, Laziness...)
35. After a heavy emotional situation, how does your body react?
36. Are you an aggressive or passive person?
37. What is the body language of your character?
38. How do you protect your feelings from showing?
39. What makes you angriest?
40. List three character failures.
41. What are your emotional triggers? (Three situations that would bring tears.)
42. What is your main goal in life?

SITUATIONAL CHARACTER QUESTIONS:

43. What is the most exciting thing that ever happened to you?
44. What is the most traumatic thing that ever happened to you?
45. What physical disease have you had? What were the effects?
46. If you could change anything about the world, what is one thing would you alter?
47. What is the most effective way of getting your own way?
48. If you could change anything in your life, what would it be?
49. How do you feel about death?
50. Describe your most recent dream.

RELATIONSHIP CHARACTER QUESTIONS:

51. Describe the first time you were intimate in any way or if you haven't been explain why not.
52. What is your perspective on intimacy?
53. Have you ever been in love? With whom and when?
54. How do you feel about each character in the play?
55. What would the other character's in the play say about you?
56. How do you get along with people in general? (Socially, Opposite Sex)

BONUS—EXPECT THE UNEXPECTED

I'll be quick here as I know this chapter threw a lot of information at you. Here's an awesome tip you might not think about until it's too late.

This industry is known for having a "hurry up and wait" mentality. This means you sit around waiting quite a bit, only to be told at the last minute that you're needed ASAP. It's fairly common to get zero notice when it comes to auditions, callbacks, set times etc. So I recommend having an emergency actor kit in your car.

Inside your kit, you should be prepared for any scenario. This should include a neutral audition outfit (something like jeans and a black T-shirt), a second outfit that suggests a working professional (a button-down shirt and slacks or skirt), a hair brush, gel or hair spray, oral care, resume, and two copies of your headshot, one commercial and one dramatic. These are in addition to those found in your actor notebook, in case you forget the notebook at home. Once your kit is assembled in your car, don't touch it unless you need it and you'll never be caught off-guard for that last minute audition.

CHAPTER 3

BUILD YOUR TEAM

"Your circle should want to see you win. Your circle should clap loudly when you have good news. If not, get a new circle."
—*Wesley Snipes*

Acting is a spectacular art form that, at its highest level, can literally change the world. An Academy Award-worthy performance in the right film at the right time has the ability to alter the way we think and behave toward one another. We get to revisit history, telling the forgotten stories of those who didn't make the cut. Actors are chosen to represent national brands in order to sell products on a massive scale. We are called upon to lighten the weight when our world feels dark. Professional actors are revered and compensated at the highest level, along with top athletes, CEOs, and politicians, and with good reason. To be an actor is an opportunity, and a responsibility, to be a light for others. It's daunting and amazing at the same time.

You'll rise as high as you're willing through hard work, determination, and support. Breaking into higher elevations will require surrounding yourself with individuals who see where you are going, believe in your vision, and support a lifestyle of what Tony Robbins calls "constant and never-ending improvement." In this chapter, we will be discussing relationships that are important to creating and maintaining a successful acting career. I'm going to guide you through the process of dealing with agents, managers, family, friends, colleagues, and coaches. Then, as a bonus, we'll finish off by pulling back the curtain on the dreaded casting directors so you'll never fear auditioning again.

1. Manage those who will be managing you

2. Customize your support system

3. Bonus—Understand the truth about casting directors

MANAGE THOSE WHO WILL BE MANAGING YOU

Choosing an agent is an important step. A good agent will advocate for and support your goals. They will open new doors, create new connections, and give guidance as you transition through different stages of your career. Note that you don't need an agent to get started, and in fact, you should begin working before you approach an agent. (Refer to Chapter One—Get Out There for more on this.) You'll want to have something on your actor resume and performance reel to demonstrate your value. Once you're ready, you should absolutely take the steps to find the right agent as soon as possible, as higher quality acting jobs usually run through SAG-accredited agencies.

Before you go on the hunt, however, understand the agent's job. Their job is to make money from helping you get work. Subtext: your agent doesn't have to be your best friend. It's fine if you build a relationship over time, but don't fool yourself. If you aren't producing income for them, you will be dropped from the agency, and, without intending to sound harsh, you should be. The relationship is only successful if it works for both parties.

Agents don't have time to work with actors who are being complacent and not landing jobs. My advice is to be patient with the process and choose the agent who demonstrates the most sincere interest in your talent. This will enable you to work more and keep you motivated to stay on your game. I recommend focusing on skill first so that you can go after the very best agent in your area, rise to become the top earner at that agency, and then work like hell to further the separation between you and everyone else in your demographic.

On the flip side of this equation, it's important you understand who works for whom. Many actors are scared of their agents, so they either cower in the corner or annoyingly suck up. Neither dynamic is appropriate. Here's the situation: your agent works for you, so technically they are contracted labor within your business. Sure, you may have to audition for them to get signed in the first place, but after that, they are then working on 100% commission; therefore, you must be professional and mature enough to understand that, while their responsibility is to present you on a pedestal, your responsibility is to ensure you have earned your agent's focus and are willing to work harder than anyone else to stay at the forefront of their mind.

Finally, remain connected to your agent by checking in periodically to see what the market is like and how they plan to get you seen. Be sure to ask if there is anything you can do on your end to make their job easier. Perhaps they would have a better chance landing you auditions if you updated your headshots or built up a particular section of your actor resume. Whatever it is, make it happen and be diligent about knowing the details of how your agent will be shopping you to the market. If it's not working out, wait until your contract expires then move on to a different agency. No excuses. It's your career, and your success is nobody's fault but your own.

*Note: Be careful not to move agents too often. Agents know each other and talk to one another. You don't want to be known as the actor who jumps all over the place. Before moving agencies make sure you have done everything you can on your end and try to maintain a positive relationship on the way out. It's good to keep doors open as the grass is not always greener on the other side of the fence.

In regard to managers and entertainment lawyers, everything above holds true. The only difference is you won't need either of these until a bit later in your career. A manager is going to help you manage all your auditions and roles. Entertainment lawyers are needed to negotiate big contracts once you've hit a level above standard rates. Agents, managers, and entertainment lawyers will all take a percentage of your acting income. So be sure you are ready and can justify taking on each of these expenses.

CUSTOMIZE YOUR SUPPORT SYSTEM

Remember how glamorously I described being an actor above? Well, there's a cost that goes with it that nobody thinks about, and most people aren't willing to pay. Once you decide to announce that this is your path, stand back and get ready for the mudslinging to begin.

It starts with your family and friends who might "lovingly" question your choice of vocation. (Refer to the fairy tale in Chapter One—Get Out There.) They will voice their often well intended concern, saying, "That's a really hard industry to get into" or "Just make sure you have a backup plan." What you're hearing is their fear: this profession is foreign to most people and therefore there is an assumption they won't be able to help you be successful. You can't just let go of your family, but you can strive to gently educate while also ignoring what is said in fear. Better yet, use their doubts as fuel to make your engine run harder. Remember, even though it may not feel this way, comments like this are generally said out of love. The same people who worry on your behalf will certainly be the ones who are bragging about you to their friends down the line. Keep the love, leave the fear.

Then there's a whole other set of people in your life to consider: those who actually do just want to take you down. This attack usually comes in the form of passive, sarcastic jabs cloaked under the guise of interest in your new endeavor. Their comments sound something like, "Wow, so you're really going to be an actor huh?" or "What have you been in that I might have seen?" or "You're still acting, huh? Good luck with that." Don't underestimate your instinct when it comes to these folks. Trust your gut. If someone feigns interest in your new career choice, and after you're done talking, the wind has been taken out of your sails, that's because they did it on purpose. These "friends" can't help themselves because they are operating from a different kind of fear: *the fear of you actually being successful at this*. In fact, this particular strain of fear might better be labeled "jealousy." As you have the courage to do something remarkable. If you continue on this path, you will be doing something you love wildly, and getting paid to do it. This is not the experience of most working adults and that makes you different. To be successful, you will have to expand beyond who you currently are at this moment and not everyone in your life will be able to make the journey. Your relationships will change over time, and you'll have to let some people go along the way. Don't be afraid of this; it's a good and natural part of progression. Make the choice to love those you leave behind exactly where they are, and then let go. Becoming a great actor is hard enough. Allow yourself to release the guilt as you won't be able to fly while carrying the weight of other people's negativity and fear.

Somehow, you're still standing after having taken the punches from both family and friends. Excellent. The final obstacle will be your colleagues, or other actors who are scratching for a piece of the same space. We touched on this group in Chapter One while discussing networking events. The reason I'm cautious of those events is that they tend to attract all the people who got into acting for the wrong reasons. People walking around with inflated egos, who prioritize self-promotion over dedication to craft. Both are important but if the former comes first, you'll end up on the stat sheet with all the other wannabe quitters.

In a commercial class I attended as a young actor, I remember the instructor dubbing this group as The Barracudas. In hindsight, the nickname rings true. You have to watch out (and even avoid these folks at all costs) because, unlike your friends and family, these people are out for blood. The Barracudas are not hard to spot once you know what to look for. At a networking event, it's the person who talks at you for a few minutes while glancing over your shoulder to see if anyone more important is nearby. In the audition room, it's an actor happy to disrupt the environment with mindless chatter (about themselves, of course), and the next thing you know, your focus is gone. Rather than working on themselves, this group of bottom feeders will attempt to draw you in, then snap you up in a feeding frenzy. The strategy is to be polite, but simply avoid them. Let them keep discussing their last gig with someone else, while you spend time working toward landing your next one. You are the only person who can ensure that you do not let others rent space in your mind. At the end of the day, be sure everything you do is in line with achieving your goals. Be strong enough not to let the roadblocks, either in the form of people or things, stand in your way.

Are you scared yet? Good. Because I never said this was easy, and a healthy fear for the process is okay. Now let's start heading toward that tiny circle of light at the end of the tunnel, shall we? You're going to need support along the way, and I promise you, *you will find it*. The key is not to settle for the default support system that life provided if it's not working for you. Instead understand that you are the architect and you have the ability to build your own custom circle of influence.

According to motivator Jim Rohn, "You are the average of the five people you spend the most time with." So who do you want to be? If you desire to be a great actor, you need to hang around great actors. If you desire to become a better version of yourself, you must connect with other people who share that mindset. Be patient with this process, and have faith that the right people will come into your life as you continue to change for the better.

I have found in my life that the concept of "like attracts like" has held true time and again. It's not a coincidence that famous actors and high level CEOs weren't knocking down the door to train with me early in my coaching career. The fact is that I hadn't earned the right to be in the same room with those people. I had to first change who I was before the people around me began to change. You will have to do the same thing. It's been my experience that as you progress forward you will have to filter out those who don't belong in order to make room for those who are meant to lift you up. The more you dream big, the more attractive you will be to other dreamers. You'll find great people in acting class, on set, or anywhere. They might be other actors and filmmakers, but they don't have to be. Anyone who is out there working to get better at their respective craft each and every day belongs on your team. Think about your areas of weakness, and seek individuals who are strong in those areas. Accountability is essential. You want people in your life who will be honest and who have your best interest at heart.

BONUS—UNDERSTAND THE TRUTH ABOUT CASTING DIRECTORS

The acting industry has gotten a certain reputation, and for good reason. It's not a secret: some bad people made their way to the top and did some bad things. They treated people poorly, and much like any other fraternity, the hazing and misconduct has been passed down through several generations. One of the worst examples of this is seen in the egotistical casting director, wielding their influence for evil. The good news is that for every bad apple out there disrupting the landscape, there are a bunch of great people working to build the industry up.

Casting directors are an important piece of the puzzle. Yet some actors have acquired a disproportionate level of fear over their approbation. The common notion is that they hold some kind of power over you, and therefore, you have to take whatever abuse they may deliver. This perception is completely false. A casting director's job is to help a producer find the right actors for their project. The process usually consists of narrowing down a large group of people into a smaller sample size in order to make the casting process easier. A good casting director will not play favorites and will not be rude. Their job is, in fact, to bring out the best in the actors they see. Any casting director who belittles or elicits fear simply isn't very good at their job.

As an actor, you don't need to be intimidated by casting directors and if you run into one who is abusive, ignore their comments. If it's bad enough, you might even choose to stop auditioning for them. The truth about casting directors is that they aren't the ones making the decision at the end of the day anyway. Casting directors gather actors and direct them through the audition process and then the producer or director will make the final decision on who gets cast for a role. The producer or director has the final say. Your job is to prepare, show up, give the best performance you can, then focus on the next audition. Don't be afraid. Don't suck up. Do your job, and move on.

*Note: It's a good idea to take a workshop or two with the local casting directors in your area. These workshops should supplement, not replace, your regular training. In these workshops, the casting director will share useful information about their personal casting philosophy, which may prove useful in future casting opportunities. You'll be given the chance to introduce yourself and hopefully learn something you didn't know.

CHAPTER 4

BRAND YOURSELF

"You have to be the best version of yourself and if that means you have to be a bit self promoting, then it's ok. It really is."
—Reese Witherspoon

The man who doesn't seem to age past forty, always sports a timeless suit that is somehow both casual and upscale, and who consistently dons the perfect blend of salt and pepper in his hair can be none other than Mr. George Clooney. The "cool girl" who magically strikes the balance between tomboy, stumbling damsel in distress, and sultry feline reminds us of Jennifer Lawrence. Wearing sunglasses indoors is as connected to Jack Nicholson as the swoosh is to Nike.

The common thread that separates those who have found a personal brand from everyone else is a mixture of self discovery and consistency. Ta-da! That's branding. You can make the excuse that you're "just you" and these celebrities have huge budgets with teams of people who work on their styling, or you can get smart and realize that behind every success story is a person who was willing to put in the work to believe in themselves before anyone else would look twice. You are a work in progress, fine, but so am I, and so is every other person walking the planet, including celebrities. Nobody has it easy. Everyone has a story and past. The question to ask yourself is not whether you're capable of having a personal brand. The question is, *What is my current brand telling the world, and is that image in alignment with my goals and dreams?* Like it or not, your personal branding has already begun to form prior to the launch of your acting career.

What would those who know you say if they had to describe your look? Your habits and character? How would they characterize the way you speak? What would your boss or teacher have to say about your daily work ethic? The answer to these questions, the honest answer, is the current status of your personal brand. You're about to start gathering information about yourself like you were a private eye investigating you. One of the most important questions you must be willing to answer is, "How am I perceived at a glance?" Or "what is the first impression I give off when walking into a room?" Some of you will be insulted at this notion. Please don't be. You know as well as I do that you are far more than your appearance. But don't pretend that the world we live in doesn't pass judgment based on looks and perception. And that's true for everyone. You can add to the equation that the acting industry is primarily a visual medium. It becomes clear real quick that your image matters.

OK, so hopefully you are sold on getting a handle on your personal branding. Now it's time to shed the insecurities and self doubt because this process can and should be fun. Working on yourself and developing consistency is empowering. You have the capacity to decide who you want to be and dedicate every day toward becoming that version of yourself. The world perceives you a certain way already, but that image can be shifted over time. Just remember that you have to be real. It's impossible to change the perception of who you are without changing what you do. In this chapter, we will discuss how to figure out your current casting type, and lean into the things that make you different. We'll discuss how social media should be used as an actor and what to avoid online to protect yourself. Finally, we will discuss your personal brand and how to consistently deliver the same message so that you leave a lasting impression.

1. Know your casting type
2. Learn to market
3. Be relentless in your consistency

KNOW YOUR CASTING TYPE

Every night at 7:30pm, I become a salesman. I try to sell my kids on the idea of going to bed: "I'll throw in one extra story and ten minutes of snuggles." (Unfortunately for me, my six-year-old is a master negotiator. But that's not the point.) Truthfully, we are all salespeople at one time or another. We sell our boss on a raise, we sell our spouse on the importance of a date night, we sell our parents on letting us drive a car. Life is all about selling yourself, and in order to do so more effectively, it's important to work on increasing your value. The best way to do this is by narrowing your focus into a concentrated niche and becoming great in that area. In the world of acting, this is your casting type. Especially when you're still working toward getting noticed, it's important to lean into your current strengths. Eventually you will have the ability to work outside this demographic, but early on, this will be the bread and butter.

Knowing and exploiting your casting type will give you an edge, and you're going to want every advantage you can get. Let's get real. Most people have to go through some sort of interview process before being hired. As an actor, you are no different, except that when you get work, it's usually for a week or less at a time. Then the process repeats and you must compete in a live interview every time you want to work. It's somewhat terrifying. I'm not going to sugarcoat anything in this book. This job is very hard, even though the joy of landing a big gig is amazing. If you're a realist, the joy only lasts about 24 hours because once that time is up, you understand that, at this point, you are officially one job away from being out of work again. Now, before you get too intimidated and walk away, know that there are many other high-pressure careers out there where people live in a state of fluctuation. Acting is high risk and high reward. You're going to get work, and when you do, the pay is usually pretty awesome. Some commercials pay thousands of dollars for just one day on set, and then continue to pay residually while the advertisement is being used. It's important that you allow yourself to celebrate the wins when they come, but always stay focused on the process of fine-tuning your skills in order to book that next job. It's not about the gig—it's about the process, progress, and growth needed to get there. (Read more on this concept in Chapter 7—Be a Great Actor.)

So, knowing the difficulties that lie ahead, let's go through the process of defining your casting type in order to narrow your focus and increase the odds of early success.

Begin by finding yourself in television shows, commercials, and movies. Be specific and honest as you search. Are you the dreamy football star? You could be the cranky neighbor upstairs, the tough-as-nails CEO, the pearl-clutching soccer mom, the best friend, the awkward teenager... you get my point. You have a "type" right now, today, exactly as you are. That type, along with your gender, race, and age, is your demographic. As you age and develop yourself, your demographic will shift, but don't go looking for work where you want to be; start with where you already are. Here's a great exercise: find three actors who seem to be taking all your work. It may take some time to pin them down, but keep digging. These might be actors who you're frequently told you resemble, or actors who seem to land roles that would be perfect for you.

It's important not to be offended by your own casting type. As I write this, I am currently 37 years old. I can't be surprised or upset that I'm not getting cast as a college student anymore. To deny reality is unproductive. Instead of holding on the past, clutching tightly to a demographic in which I used to land a lot of roles in, I prefer to spend my time getting paid to be the best "dad" type I can be. From here I can branch into fun, goofy or serious disciplined dad. Narrowing my focus in actuality has the effect of defining a new niche from which I can thrive. The niche developed also opens opportunities to land roles that are similar such as CEO, police officer or store manager. By doing this I have landed more roles with less effort than I did in my twenties. I strongly advise that you do the same. As mentioned above, film and television rely on visual storytelling. Think about how fast a commercial moves. Consider the quick, snappy cuts required for a sitcom. We don't always have the luxury of time. The audience needs to be able to gather information about a character (you) quickly, just at a glance. So take a good look at yourself in the mirror. Do this without fear, without judgment. Ask yourself what makes you different. *Where would I be seen on television?*

Actress Beth Grant is a great example of this process in action. You may or may not have heard her name before, but that doesn't matter. You'd probably know her face instantly, and more importantly, she's been busy doing what she loves for decades. Beth Grant is a busy working actress and a major success story. At the advice of an acting coach, she wisely narrowed her focus away from the leading lady demographic and into "proletariat, salt-of-the-earth" (a fancy way of saying her look represented the average person, not the hero). Turns out her coach was right, in that soon after she shifted into her natural demographic, Beth Grant landed a role in the movie Rain Man with Dustin Hoffman. Of course, she had already cultivated her talent by that point in her career, but identifying her casting type was the missing piece. Before stepping into her casting type, Beth Grant had eight actor credits on IMDB over a span of ten years. Today she has 222 and counting.

I know there is something special about you because there is something special about everyone. We all have our own DNA and unique set of fingerprints. Often, the thing you are trying to hide will become your biggest asset if you are brave enough to share it with the world. Imagine an actor who is afraid to highlight his name, features, and ethnicity for fear of being looked at as a terrorist. Then take Punjabi actor Anil Kapoor, who has used and perfected an image that landed him a role as a terrorist on the show *24* with Kiefer Sutherland. When looking at Anil's career, we don't see a terrorist but a skilled craftsman who can play a terrorist and just about any other character thrown his way. Anil Kapoor has over 120 credits, including the award winning *Slumdog Millionaire*, *Mission Impossible*, and even an episode of *Family Guy*. You are who you are, and it's OK to be that person. Just be sure to work at getting better each and every day. As soon as you settle, your career is over. At the same time, you must become the best version of YOU! Not somebody else. You are the uniquely wonderful combination of *your* age, *your* height, *your* weight, *your* ethnicity. No one can reproduce you again exactly as you are. You have to see and understand how beautiful that makes you. When this ceases to be head knowledge and seeps into the fabric of your heart, you'll be amazed at how much easier acting (and life) becomes. Acting from who you are will open doors and provide an opportunity to gain experience as you continue to master the craft. (We will talk about mastery later in Chapter 7—Be a Great Actor. Spoiler alert: There are no shortcuts.)

Note: The exception to the rule above would be any project or creative team that opposes your personal values and beliefs.

LEARN TO MARKET

Once you get your first agent, if you haven't already, you will quickly discover what a big deal it isn't. Having an agent is great, but once you reach that milestone, you better have a plan to market yourself. Agents can't and won't do all the work for you. An agent will, of course, send you out on auditions that come their way; however, they simply don't have time to act as a manager for their entire roster of talent. There aren't enough hours in the day for them to hunt down specific work for you (and the hundreds of faces they represent) to gain experience and exposure. You want to take your success into your own hands and avoid being dead weight.

Any business owner or salesperson will tell you that sitting back and waiting for customers is a surefire way to ensure you don't have any. Make no mistake about it: you are your own product, and you need people to see your value in order to eventually pay for it.

So who are your customers? Producers, filmmakers, cinematographers and directors, for a start. We touched on creating relationships at networking events already, (See Chapter One—Get Out There) but promoting yourself and having an online presence is equally essential. In all your marketing, be sure to stay consistent with your brand and messaging, it will be easier for your clients to spot and remember you for future work. Which leads to the "how" part of actor marketing.

Actors should have the following basic tools at their disposal to properly market themselves: headshots by an experienced photographer, an actor website and corresponding email list, a demo reel, thank-you cards, and a professional social media presence. All of these tools need to be updated consistently, particularly your social media. Otherwise, you can't expect results.

Your website doesn't need to be incredibly flashy to start, but it should be professional. Don't be afraid to create your own if hiring a designer is out of your budget. You should make sure to have a page with your current actor resume, easy links to your social media, and a page for your actor demo reels and video footage. Keep an email list with subcategories, and give people a place to opt-in on your website. Be sure to add to this by taking down the contact information of those you work with in order to keep in touch. (See Chapter 2—Get Organized.) I would suggest sending out a quarterly email to everyone on the list with updates on your progression as an actor. This is a great time to highlight others you have worked with and those who have hired you. Personal emails should be sent directly after you have worked with or been in contact with anyone whom you wish to work with again. Create a strategic follow-up plan for each contact based on the circumstance in order to keep yourself fresh on their mind. Plan based on their perceived needs, stay organized and execute. For example, when you finish your part in a movie, you should immediately follow up with an email and thank you letter the very next day. If the crew is still in production, it's likely that message will not get a response. The recipient will be grateful for the gesture but probably won't have the time to respond. A good strategy would be to then write a follow-up personal email that is scheduled to go out one week after production is complete. At the same time, this contact will have been added to your general email list and will see in your next quarterly email that they are being highlighted. At this point, you will have made contact three times over the span of six to nine months. Guess how long it generally takes to move from one project to the next? That's right, six to nine months! By keeping in touch with former clients in this way, you increase your chances for repeat business with directors and producers who know and trust your work. A direct booking (being hired as an actor without auditioning) saves the client money and time, and it's a huge win for the actor!

As far as social media is concerned, you already know about all the tools available at your fingertips to market yourself. Actors are now free to promote themselves with unprecedented ease. This gives us ways to connect that actors have never dreamed of before, and the innovations are going to compound in the coming years. In fact there are so many tools available that becoming overwhelmed with too many options has become the greatest obstacle. So my advice here is to narrow your focus based on your brand and demographic. It's better to be great on one platform than to be mediocre on ten.

The social media evolution is a great way for aspiring actors to market if they know what they're doing. It's time, if you haven't done this already, to get yourself a professional page on a few of the top platforms, and then to either drop your personal profiles or make them private. You don't need me to tell you this, but you would be surprised just how many people will be looking at your social profiles when you are auditioning, being called back, or booking a job. Do yourself a favor and present yourself as a professional on all accounts, quite literally. Casting directors are looking for people who can sell a product and represent an idea, message, theme, or product. Don't give them a reason to drop you because of social media. Use it to promote your talent and further define your brand! You then need to dedicate yourself to using each platform with intention. You are the marketing director of your own company, so become a student in this craft ASAP and get active. Don't write this off as a "young person's game." For all demographics, having a social media presence is slowly becoming as important as the headshot.

Admittedly I am not an expert in this subject, though I am working on it daily. I suggest you become a student in this area as well. Go take some classes, and learn from people who are out there doing only that one thing. There's no shortage of people out there right now writing books and producing podcasts on the subject of social media but I am hesitant to recommend specific sources as the landscape seems to be shifting too fast to keep up. The basic message here is to make sure you are informed without getting overwhelmed. (Having said that, visit www. DearingStudio.com/ActingIsMyDayJob for an updated list of social strategy resources.)

BE RELENTLESS IN YOUR CONSISTENCY

Once you get a clear picture of what your demographic currently is and have decided on a strategy to put yourself out there, consistency is king. As an actor, your image is your livelihood, so get specific with the exact "vibe" you wish to convey, and then stick to it. Are you trendy, pursuing to-the-minute accessories and styles? Casual and easy? Timeless and tailored? Take the time to pin it down. Of course, your style, like your demographic, will change over time. I'm not saying you need to wear the same three outfits for the rest of your life; however, you will benefit from figuring out the most flattering color palette and styles for you. Not only will you feel more confident, but you'll also begin to create an easily recognizable "product." Maybe begin by garnering the help of those around you, and use free resources to help you figure out what exactly will bring out the best of your physical side, so your mind can keep grinding toward the dream. Takeaway here: the more consistent you are with your image, the easier it is to be remembered.

Ask yourself this question: would an impressionist comedian be able to create an impersonation of you based on the last 30 posts you put up on various social media platforms? Do you have a clearly defined way of communicating and styling yourself? This should be your goal, to get to a place where you own a certain way of dressing and interacting. If you are consistent, any time someone dresses similar to you, it will be seen by others as if they are trying to look like you. Pay attention to those with the most recognizable personal brands. Yes, they will often keep up with current styles, but notice how consistent they are with their language, posture, and certain elements of their personal style. Even someone who appears to not care about their look, but who does so on a consistent basis, is making a choice to brand themselves in that way. Branding is all about repetition so lean into who you are and be relentless in your consistency.

CHAPTER 5

BE A PRODUCER

"If opportunity doesn't knock, build a door." —*Milton Berle*

I'm not the first to say this, and I won't be the last: this industry requires thick skin. Better yet, a coat of armor. It's very common for actors to hear "no" over one hundred times before getting to their first "maybe." It can be maddening if you are not prepared for that kind of rejection. Actor success is a long game that requires patience. Being an actor isn't a safe job with the guarantee of hours, benefits, and vacation time. If it were, everyone would have this job because, let's be honest, being an actor is awesome. Wait a minute, didn't I mention in the introduction of this book that you shouldn't be scared of the industry dragon? That's true, and I stand by that statement, but I never said the dragon doesn't exist. There is a dragon, and he is ferocious. The only thing to take notice of is that there is a dragon hidden in every profession. The lie is that becoming a professional actor requires different work than becoming great at anything else. To be great at anything takes skill that can only be acquired over time through diligently working on your craft. You'll find this point made throughout the book and hammered home in Chapter 7—Be a Great Actor because it's the most important ingredient to your success.

So how *do* you overcome the industry dragon? The stinging rejection of multiple callbacks resulting in another "no"? The pain of running into wall after wall without giving up? It's simple. **You cast yourself.** You stop waiting, and start doing. You put the power back into your own hands and stop making excuses. Success is not something delivered in the mailbox. If you spend your time sitting on the couch watching other people living out your dreams, what do you think is going to happen? You must take action! Part of the reason we're drawn to acting is that we love great stories. You have an amazing untold story inside your heart, dying to get out. I know you do. You know you do, too, so write the script. Test it out. Find a film student and shoot it. You do it. Right now, today. If you truly want to be successful, you need start creating content yourself.

Will you fail a few times? More than a few. Will your first projects be so bad you're embarrassed to even show your mother? Yep, probably. Will you make money at some point from creating your own content? Maybe, maybe not. You might have something to say that the market loves, and you may find yourself making a living on YouTube. Either of those options would be happy accidents. But that's not why I'm telling you to do it. The reason to produce is because it fills that creative hole inside and reminds us why we started acting in the first place. Your own productions will be a safe place to experiment, have fun, and get better. Worst-case scenario: you'll begin building an audience and stretching yourself as a performer. There is absolutely nothing to lose in the art of practice. If you stick with the process long enough and you provide valuable content, the money will follow, either directly or indirectly. In this chapter, we will discuss how to get started, what to produce, and how to build a following.

1. Start with what you've got

2. Produce a show

3. Build a following

START WITH WHAT YOU'VE GOT

At the end of this section, I'm going to provide a link that will list some basic equipment that won't break the bank but will significantly increase the production value of your projects. But first, I recommend using the tools that are already at your disposal in order to eliminate the excuses for not getting started. To quote Arnold Schwarzenegger, "You can have results or excuses. Not both." If you wait until all the conditions are perfect or until you feel like an expert, you'll probably never do the thing you've always wanted to do.

The good news is that you don't have to wait another second to get started. If you have a smartphone, you've already got a pretty decent camera and microphone sitting in your pocket. My guess is that you also have some sort of computing device, or at least access to one, which means you have the ability to type words. There you go. You've just overcome the excuse of a financial barrier holding you back from scriptwriting and producing.

I get it. You technically *could* produce, but should you? I mean, using a phone isn't going to deliver great quality right? True. Here's my take on the subject. It's okay if these look low-budget at first. They are low-budget. First of all, social media is designed for quick and raw entertainment, so in that way, your "raw" take will be admired. Understanding that you have limits in production should also help you to raise the standards of the actual content itself. This will force you to fight for only the best, most entertaining or impactful content. So just go out and create. If you don't love the end product, then don't put it out. Consider that failed attempt to be part of your training. Once you have a premise you like, you can use your existing marketing platform to push it out to the world! Since the landscape is always changing, research the different platforms before launching your idea. For instance, at the moment, Facebook is a fantastic place to try out two- to three-minute videos. Because it's a sharing platform, great content can get you a wide reach in a short time. YouTube is great for longer content, where people settle in to really go deeper on a topic or to binge-watch a favorite entertainer. A thirty-second "tease" of your sketch or a funny meme from a still frame is perfect for Instagram. Understand that the media outlets mentioned here are all competing with each other and will make adjustments to do so. It's important you keep an eye on new updates and shifts in the market so you don't end up with all your content on something like MySpace. Never heard of MySpace? That's my point. Each platform has something unique to offer to help with the distribution of your content. Don't be quick to dismiss any of them, and remain diligent in exploring the new technology available at your fingertips.

No excuses are allowed, which is why you heard me tell you to start on your phone, and I meant it. But only stay there as long as you need to. As soon as you can upgrade your equipment (or hire a videographer), do it. You want to create a great experience for the audience you're working so hard to build. Much like not being afraid to audition, the same holds true for creating content. It's better to make an imperfect first impression, as long as you continue to develop and get better. Your audience will appreciate the higher quality as you gradually learn to produce with the equipment you can afford. Upgrade when possible and only as needed. You will find an updated list of basic equipment you will need to take your productions to the next level at www. DearingStudio.com/ActingIsMyDayJob.

Note: All items listed have huge price variables have huge price variables based on quality. I suggest buying based on your needs and to make sure to always maximize your current equipment before investing in upgrades.

PRODUCE A SHOW

Now it's time to think about the content you want to produce! There are no hard and fast rules here, so the sky's the limit. You can create anything your heart desires on any platforms that are interesting to you. This is both good and bad. The issue with too many options is that the act of simply choosing can end up feeling overwhelming and can once again hold you back. If you can't immediately think of a brilliant idea, don't be discouraged. The best bet, once again, is to just begin the process and start from who you are and what you already know. The good news is that you probably know more than you think you do.

Let's start with the possibility of creating a comedic character as an idea. Actress and singer Colleen Ballinger began creating content with her creation of the character Miranda Sings. This character was originally inspired by some of her classmates while she was studying as a vocal performance major. The character represented those in her industry who were rude to others while waiting for their fame. For years, she has patiently developed the inept singer who had unwavering faith in her vocal brilliance. The result is absolutely hysterical, and success has followed. The character eventually gained so much popularity she went on national tours, wrote bestselling books and landed her own Netflix series, *Haters Back Off.* The point of this story is to see what is possible, and to give perspective on where to start. Colleen knew about singing. She knew about being a student singer and what that crowd was like. She created from what she knew and remained consistent in her pursuit. Success didn't happen overnight; it took many years, and the actress is still today producing videos and challenging herself to stay relevant. If you are interested, take a look at the quality of videos and depth of the character from ten years ago until now. The progress is staggering, but in order to get to where she is, Colleen Ballinger had to be brave enough to take an unpolished idea and put it out there.

Maybe you have a character like Miranda Sings you've been using to entertain your family and friends. Perhaps you do a fantastic impression of your great Aunt Dee. Perfect. Use that as a starting point to be exaggerated, developed, and put in different situations to create comedic gold. Maybe you don't even have a fully formed character yet, but you do have a funny voice your nephew and niece just love. All you need is a seed! Start there! A great way to develop or discover characters is to jump into an improv class. You'll get a chance to test out some of your ideas on stage while collaborating with other creative artists. You'll get feedback on what really hits and what doesn't from both the student audience and your instructor. As you try to learn more about the character you're creating, ask good questions. Go to www.DearingStudio.com/ActingIsMyDayJob for our handout on Good Character Questions. (This is the bonus worksheet found in Chapter 2 - Get Organized)

Maybe you don't have an interest in comedy. No problem. Ask yourself what you care deeply about. What issues, platforms, and people do you know a lot about? What is a subject that excites you? What makes your blood boil? If you can patiently unearth the things that you're most passionate about, you'll find a wellspring of writing material and potential ideas. This could end up manifesting in writing a short film, speaking straight to camera, launching a podcast, or creating a web show.

Another good angle is to become the expert in something that interests you. In doing so, you don't have to be an *actual* expert; you just have to be willing to be honest and teach others what they don't already know. In fact, people often love to watch someone else in the learning process as long as that person is willing to share along the way. We know you're hooked on acting, but do you also enjoy putting outfits together? Do you play an instrument? Do you whittle tiny sloths out of driftwood and sell them on Etsy? The point is, I'll bet there's something of value that you have to talk about. And if you know something I don't and you're willing to share that information with me, you have just become valuable in my eyes. While I realize this isn't the same thing as writing a movie, it's still very much a creative endeavor. You'll have to write and think things through. You're still logging hours in front of the camera or microphone. And don't you dare tell me you have nothing to talk about. If you're a human, you have things to talk about. Use the voice you have to get yourself on camera and create content that you care about. You'll grow as an artist, and the world will thank you for your efforts.

Now that the wheels are turning, it will be wise to narrow down what you create, at least in the beginning, to things that are consistent with your branding decisions. Let's say, for instance, that you're an actress in the young mom demographic. As an extension of your casting type, it would make logical sense for you to film videos about parenting. You create lots of content about ways to deal with tantrums, sibling fights, being a working mom, peaceful sleeping habits for the family, etc. For this actor, it would make much less sense to post videos about going out to the club to get crazy. Maybe some social media personalities would disagree with me here, but this feels like common sense. Of course you want to let your audience get to know you, and authenticity is important, but remember why people are visiting you in the first place. If you stay on or close to your branding then future clients who see your work will already be primed to hire you in that demographic.

Creating your own content is satisfying, and the better you get at the process, the more addictive it becomes. You'll find ways to cross-promote over different platforms, and before you know it, people will be clamoring to be on the next episode of your show.

And speaking of guests, self-produced content is also a great time to tap into the new network you are building for yourself. Acting class is a great place to cast your projects. Seek to work with those you admire and who work the hardest. The hardest working people will push you to be better and that's who you want running next to you. As a final note, you'd be surprised how hard it can be for student filmmakers to find dedicated actors who are good and willing to work for free. See if you can negotiate a trade that benefits both parties. Offer to donate your time to be talent at your nearest film school on a few projects in exchange for videography services for your next big idea.

BUILD A FOLLOWING

Once you are creating new, on-brand and interesting content, the next step is to build your following. In order to do this, consistency is vital. Getting out there and doing "something" is always better than sitting around thinking about it. But once you get going, pick a schedule and stick to it. If you want to be a professional actor, you have to treat acting like it is a profession. Your weekly podcast or comedy sketch is not an option, it's your job. What happens if you don't show up to work? That's right, you get fired. People love the underdog story. They will forgive your lack of experience and quality in order to feel like they are a part of some underground movement. Just look at the Miranda Sings story from earlier in this chapter. But they will not forgive you if you fail to show up or don't deliver on a promised deadline. In the earliest days of our acting school, we performed improv shows for audiences of eight or nine people, most of whom were friends and family. The shows were every Friday night at 7PM and our "theater" was a small lobby inside a doctor's office. Trust me, there were many nights we didn't want to be there. But guess what? We showed up and we gave those few people the best show we were capable of at the time. Ten years later, that show is still going in a real theater and for much larger crowds. We've traveled across the country to perform, won several awards, and get paid top dollar to entertain in corporate environments.

The point is to progress forward no matter what and to give everything you have as if you already were at your dream destination. Eventually, through being consistent and showing an evolution of growth in content and quality, your audience will begin to grow. This will happen slowly and organically, which is good. That's the best way to grow. You'd much rather have a hundred social media followers who are engaged and excited for your next post than ten thousand followers you bought. The one hundred engaged people are way more valuable than the ten thousand who don't care about you or your product. As your organic audience gets larger, so will your influence. Focus on providing real value, and your fans will show up when you need them to take action.

In today's landscape, until you are a household name, it is not uncommon for producers to measure your value based on digital influence. If you create a piece of content and get 20% of your audience to engage in conversation, you are killing it. If you're creating strong content that resonates, don't be surprised if someone wants to pay you to have their product sitting on your desk or to integrate taking a sip of their new soft drink in the middle of your next sketch. It's amazing. And if that doesn't happen? Who cares?! You're building your brand while working on your craft. Trust the process, and success will follow.

CHAPTER 6

RUN THE BUSINESS

"The road to success is through commitment." —*Will Smith*

Congratulations! You are officially an entrepreneur. Now you get to figure out what life is really like for the business owners who get to make their own hours. A hard reality check for most people who go out on their own comes in the form of a question: *What do I do now?* It's the same as that feeling when you graduated college and sprinted head-first into the "real world." No more classes, homework assignments, or exams! Look at you fly! Then, after a few weeks you discover that, without the pressures of a professor and curriculum demanding that you improve every day, it's not so easy to stay motivated. The cushy job you had envisioned doesn't pay what you thought it would. Oh yeah, and your student loans have officially begun accruing interest. Congratulations, and welcome to being an adult!

The joy of being your own boss is that nobody will tell you where to go or what to do. The burden of being your own boss is that nobody will tell you where to go or what to do. Make no mistake: if you are an actor, you are running your own small business. It's going to be a lifetime of trial and error. One day you will feel on top of the world, and the very next day you will question if you have what it takes. This chapter is all about the business of acting. I'm going to guide you through what it will take to begin on a solid foundation, where to invest your capital, and how to strategically turn one-time customers into repeat business you can count on.

1. You are a start up
2. Invest in the business
3. Aim for happy, repeat customers

YOU ARE A START-UP

The small business start-up has been fantasized over the last few decades after the monumental success of companies such as Microsoft, Apple, and Facebook. To be involved in a start-up company suddenly gave you cache. It had cool factor. That hype died off a bit after the tech bubble burst in 2001, but has seen a resurgence recently with the vast success of various social media platforms. Start-ups themselves are not good or bad, but you should understand what they entail before beginning yours.

There's a reason people have been starry-eyed over the start-up. They're thrilling to watch. Often the companies that "make it" are driven by serious innovators—earth-shakers challenging the status quo in one way or another. Industry titans get comfortable and stop innovating. Customers are stuck overpaying for substandard goods and services. Then the start-up enters the arena like David, fearlessly marching to meet Goliath with a slingshot in hand.

So how does this happen? How does a small idea become something big that will appeal to the masses? And how do you leverage this information when starting your own company? The answer is found is a few business fundamentals that apply across the board, including the solo actor entrepreneur. Every successful business begins with a clear vision, mission, and values that tie together in perfect harmony. As an actor, you need to go through the process of writing your own vision, mission, and values statements, and then use that information to inform every decision you make.

As we define each, I'll also give examples from our acting school. It's important to note, however, that our school is not in the business of becoming an actor. We are in the business of helping others become actors. I will tie some ideas back to you as an actor, but I don't want to give you too much here as this is a personal process, and it's important that the ideas are your own. You must believe with your whole heart in what you write down, or it won't become a reality. Here's a quick breakdown for those who didn't go to business school; don't worry, I didn't either.

A vision statement is a declaration of where you plan to be. It's not where you are but rather where you are going.

Example Vision Statement:

Dearing Acting Studio will be a respected worldwide brand and positive influence in each market we serve through our ability to connect the art of acting with personal development. We will be known for our dedication to service, innovative leadership, inspiring residential courses, unmatched virtual training programs and "light" driven content creation and distribution.

A mission statement defines what you do and what makes you different from your competition.

Example Mission Statement:

Our mission at Dearing Acting Studio is to inspire others to act with passion and realize their true potential as human beings through connecting personal development with mastery level training in the art of acting.

Values statements represent your principles, beliefs, and core values.

Example Value Statements:

In all areas of life, we are committed to act with PASSION.

LOVE is at the center of everything we do.

We live in a constant state of progression through a never-ending pursuit of MASTERY.

As you can see in the above example, your vision, mission and values should all compliment one another. They help keep you motivated and focused. So now let's briefly apply this to you as an actor. Your vision may be to make a positive impact in the entertainment industry. Your mission could be to improve daily in mind, body, and spirit while using the craft of acting to be an inspiration for positive change in the world. And your values statements could then clearly define that you will not be willing to sacrifice your artistic point of view by selling out to a project that has negative intentions. This type of clarity will make decision-making much easier as your career moves forward and you gain more influence. Tough decisions you may not think about until it's too late will include such things as what projects to audition for, who you are willing to work with, what language you are comfortable using, and what physical boundaries you absolutely will not cross. The point here is to expect success to come your way and already have those choices made in advance so you'll never be tempted to compromise your values.

This process will essentially get you to the "why" of your business. Once you know your "why," you'll be armed with the strength it will take to get through the first few years. You'll probably have to keep a second job until the checks start coming in with regularity. You can expect criticism along the way, even from people who love you. Running your own business will take grit and an indomitable determination, but anyone is capable of this. It's just a matter of saying "yes, I can" and "quitting is not an option." And it really won't be an option to quit if you have a strong enough "why" to keep you going.

INVEST IN THE BUSINESS

Every start-up needs a little capital to get it off the ground, and the acting business is no different. There are some basic things you will need right away, and there are other helpful tools that can wait until after the first couple of paychecks come. We'll discuss both of these in this section.

Before you do anything else, find an accountant to help you set up an LLC for your acting career. This is essential so that you will be able to track income and write-off expenses. (More on this in Chapter 2—Get Organized.) This will save you a lot of money and allow you to take advantage of potential losses from the first few years. Then the groundwork will be laid, and you'll learn to manage the money you will eventually make.

The first investment you should make, after setting up the LLC, is in yourself. As an actor, you are the product you are selling; therefore, working on yourself and the craft of acting is like buying inventory. Be sure to always be in an acting class with a coach who is challenging. The acting classes you take at any level should encourage growth and hold you accountable for making progress. (More on this in Chapter 7—Be a Great Actor.)

Next, you should have a gym membership or (at minimum) a health and fitness plan that you are committed to. Actors come in every shape and size, so it has nothing to do with body type and everything to do with performing at your best. Acting requires energy, and lots of it. Have you ever watched a Broadway performance? Those are athletes, people. Your body is the instrument you are playing, and you have nothing else to hide behind. It is essential that you keep your instrument finely tuned at all times. Along these same lines, I strongly recommend working with a vocal coach as soon as you can afford to do so. Until then, do your best to practice on your own by reading and watching tutorials on improving your voice. These resources are free and will at least allow you to start laying a solid foundation.

You should also get headshots taken by a seasoned photographer to help you market yourself as soon as possible. To start, you may need to be modest in how much you spend on pictures, and that's fine;however, once you can afford to do so, be selective and take the time to really examine the work of those you are considering. A good photographer will know how to showcase an individual's uniqueness. The professional you choose must understand the difference between an actor headshot and a beautiful picture. A good picture is fine and good, but the point of the headshot is to sell the actor. Ask your agent or acting coach for recommendations. Once your pictures have been taken and approved, have them professionally printed from a trusted online source. Personal printers and local business printers are not recommended. The digital file chosen should then be used on all marketing material, your website, and as your profile picture on all professional social pages. The professionally printed hard copies will be used to hand out at auditions.

As your business grows and your career begins to take off, you can look into further investments in the following areas: quality video and sound equipment for self tapes and auditioning, higher quality headshots, top-tier training, a demo reel, an actor website, and a bookkeeper.

AIM FOR HAPPY, REPEAT CUSTOMERS

The actor is a commodity that is bought by the highest bidder and used as a tool for that bidder to make a profit of some kind. This is why you must know who you are, which is what you are selling, and how to best position yourself to be the best option available in the niche you carve out for yourself. We spoke earlier about how difficult it is to break into this business, but also how, in many ways, it's much like any other commission-based job. To ease the stress as you continue to progress, you'll want to aim not just to serve your customer, but also to far exceed their expectations in order have them purchase your services again.

In order to exceed the expectations of your customer as an actor, you need to begin with superior preparation. Make sure you are well memorized and coached for the role you are being asked to play. Get a professional coach to make sure you understand all the nuances of your script and hopefully help you bring a little something special to the set. Have scripts, location, timesheets, and production contact information printed and appropriately placed into your actor binder. Keep your health routine by eating right, working out, and sleeping well the day before you shoot. Arrive on set *at least* a half hour earlier than your call time. This ensures that unforeseen events won't keep you from being on time. It may also not be a bad idea to test out your transportation plan by traveling to the location beforehand so you can plan out your path and avoid having to rely on your hopefully working GPS to get you to the right place on time. In a worst-case scenario, you'll have extra time to become acclimated with the set you will be working on.

Once you have prepared and find yourself on set, remember you're on a job. This means you handle yourself at all times as a professional who is focused on craft and does not get distracted by other actors or production crew. A good director and producer will take notice of both the talkers and the doers. Your job is to remain in a state of readiness at all times because acting on a set is a game of hurry up and wait. I was once in a film with Will Ferrell (I had one line), and they had me waiting around for ten hours. It was exhausting having to be ready that whole time. I thought past a certain point that my part was going to be pushed back, but then right as the shoot was about to end for the day, suddenly I was rushed to set to deliver my line. The sun was about to set, and I had literally one chance to get it right. That's just how it goes in this business. So stay alert and quiet so you can hyper-focus and listen. Then, when your number is called, go in there and leave it all on the set. Give your best performance, be respectful, and leave. It's important not to get caught up in going out too often with other actors from set or with the production crew during a shoot. The occasional outing is, of course, OK, but just realize that those late hours could cost you preparation time the next morning. Relationship-building is wonderful, but your first responsibility is to be an actor known for doing their job excellently. I'm not saying it's bad to go out, have some fun every now and then, but stay focused.

After the final day of filming, be sure to thank everyone. Sometimes, production companies send out a contact sheet before filming. If they didn't, don't leave without getting contact information of the key players on set. (I always like to get a contact for the first and second Assistant Directors so I have multiple avenues to follow up.) A few days later, send individual emails or handwritten notes thanking everyone for having you on this project. I'm not kidding about this. My wife filmed a Superbowl commercial in 2010 that featured Joan Rivers. Leeann was on contract with this particular company, so she was able to talk with the production crew the following week. They informed her that Joan Rivers had sent a handwritten note to each and every one of them. That type of kindness does not go unnoticed. In fact, it becomes your calling card. Take the chance that you may be remembered for your kindness and gratitude.

If you can, connect with each person on your social networks so they can see your ongoing work and become even more familiar with your brand. Ask permission first, then post something on all your channels that highlights the production and the product, not yourself. If you've done all these things, believe me, you have left a lasting impression, and any follow-up communication should be welcome.

This brings me to the final step: create a conversation schedule in order to check in about once every 4-6 months. When you check in, work on building relationships with no expectation or agenda. Once you've done this process with 10-20 clients, you'll begin to reap the benefits of all your hard work and consistent communication.

The goal for any business is to make money. You must have a strong reason for doing what you do, but at the end of the day, the purpose is to earn a living. There's nothing wrong with that. It may feel a little weird the first time you receive a huge payday for doing something you love and just a short time ago would have done for free, but get over that feeling quickly so you don't end up sabotaging yourself. If you run your career like a business and have the wherewithal to grind through both the good and the bad, I guarantee you will find success and the money that comes with it.

CHAPTER 7

BE A GREAT ACTOR

"Wanting to be a good actor is not good enough. You must want to be a GREAT actor. You just have to have that." — Gary Oldman

Here is where the rubber meets the road. Expect to be paid exactly what you are worth to the market. An actor's value is measured primarily upon perceived talent. Are you talented? How talented are you? While there is a subjective quality to these questions, let's discuss some helpful guideposts for evaluating something of far greater importance. Something that *is* within your control: skill. How much skill have you acquired? Be honest with yourself and no matter where you are, make the choice to get better. Increase your skill on a daily basis through repetition until difficult tasks become easy. For it is the ease with which we perform a skill that the untrained eye will perceive as talent.

Will Smith attributes none of his success to talent.

"No matter how talented you are, your talent will fail you, if you're not skilled. Skill is achieved through practice. Work hard and dedicate yourself to being better every single day." —Will Smith

Famed acting coach Uta Hagen describes acting talent as a list of attributes that can be developed over time.

"Talent is an amalgam of high sensitivity; easy vulnerability; high sensory equipment (seeing, hearing, touching, smelling, tasting—intensely); a vivid imagination as well as a grip on reality; the desire to communicate one's own experience and sensations, to make oneself heard and seen."
—*Uta Hagen*

The point here is that these people understand there truly is no magic bullet that will make you a great actor overnight. Nobody is "born with it," and anyone *can* acquire the skills needed to be great. These skills are not easy to come by, but anyone can learn. Everyone, and that means you too, has the capacity for talent. For the sake of this chapter, we'll use "talent" to mean your collective skills as they relate to performing arts: command over your voice, breath, movement, diction, confidence, stage presence, comedic timing, etc. All of the elements necessary for a well trained, flexible actor.

Now before we dive in, I will admit that not one of us is created equal. Life is not necessarily "fair." And obviously, some people will have certain God-given attributes that might provide an early advantage. These things might be a symmetrical face or a pair of deep blue eyes. But don't kid yourself for a second into thinking the world of acting is a "piece of cake" just because someone has a pretty face. A great physique or additional skill learned early in life might also give a leg up. These items, however, fall into the skill acquired through hard work category. So if you think that particular skill or body type will serve your career, then go out and get the skill yourself.

Here's an example of a previously acquired skill translating into perceived actor "talent". Suppose two fifteen-year-old girls begin acting at the same time. Neither of them have taken a single acting class, but one of the two has eight years' worth of performance dance training. She would likely begin the process with more perceived "talent" than the other. Her dance training offers some tangential benefits for her acting. This may be a stage presence that the other girl wouldn't have yet. It could come across in her ability to trust her body and physical choices to communicate an emotional state. This doesn't mean the girl without dance training shouldn't be an actress, of course. And it doesn't mean that the dancer is better suited or has more potential to be a great actor. It simply means the girl with dance training has acquired a complementary skill, which gives her a starting point advantage. If the young girl with dance experience quits her actor training because she has fallen for the trap of believing she is naturally "talented", the other young girl will eventually catch up and blow right past her.

Talent is not a trait gifted to the fortunate few. Talent is earned through acquiring skill. In this chapter, we will squash the myth that some people 'have it' and others do not. We'll lay down the pathway for you to release your fear and insecurity about whether or not you can actually do this. This chapter is about grit. It's about being honest with yourself and rising into your own potential. It's about changing your mindset for good, enabling you to form new success habits that serve as the beginning of the never-ending pursuit of mastery.

1. Become a student for life
2. Create good habits
3. Pursue mastery

BECOME A STUDENT FOR LIFE

I've been asked before, "When will I be good enough to stop training all the time?" All this question does is expose the immaturity of a new performer. It's laughable, but not unusual, for an actor to take a class just to put the instructor or facility on their resume. Then they move on as if the "training box" has been checked off their to-do list. Acting is an artform that *cannot be perfected*. It's one of the reasons why some of the most elite human beings on the planet are drawn to the craft. If you want to make real money as an actor and have a lasting career, surrender yourself to a lifetime of learning. It is absolutely true that agents, casting directors, and "the industry" want to see that you are training consistently at a high level. But if you are doing it for them, you are doing it for the wrong reasons, and you may need to do some work to clear the clouds away from your intentions. If you want this career, you will want and crave the high-level training that will be hard, grueling, and transformative. The kind of training that comes with growing pains. You see, this is where the mastery happens. Maybe it's on a big stage in a fancy theater, or maybe it's in a black box with a coach who believes in you and will fight to make you better. You want to be around people who will hold a mirror up to your flaws and give you the tools to take your talent to the next level. It's time to get excited about getting knocked down time after time because the act of getting up is what will make you stronger. Anyone who has achieved greatness, in any field, knows what I'm talking about. Once you're on top, you have to train harder and dig even deeper. Leonardo DiCaprio has a personal acting coach. Tom Brady has a personal coach. Oprah Winfrey has a coach.

It's time right now to change your mindset away from "When will I be good enough to stop training?" Instead, ask, "How can I get just 1% better today?"

Imagine a neurosurgeon who studied just enough to get an A on her final exam. Can she stop training at that point? Doesn't she still need to keep up with the latest techniques and technology? Of course she does. In fact you, as her potential customer who might one day require brain surgery, would demand that to be the case. If you demand that type of excellence from other professionals, shouldn't you also demand it of yourself? Shouldn't the people who might hire you as an actor have the right to demand that you be at the top of your ability at all times? The best in the world at anything know what others refuse to admit: there is always room for improvement. Does this sound discouraging? Don't let it. This should be the most freeing bit of news you receive. Understand that happiness lives in the progress. So choose to be happy now by committing to a more disciplined pursuit of your dreams. The pursuit of mastery, the incessant, tiny steps to becoming better is what you should chase after. Not the agent, the booking, or the award. It's all about progress. And if progress is your ultimate goal, those other recognizable achievements will fall into place.

I've personally paid close attention to the career of Duane Johnson, the actor and former WWF wrestler known as The Rock. It's quite difficult to be taken seriously as an actor when you've already become famous for bashing in heads while wearing tight underwear. So as Johnson began to transition, I was curious as to whether he would crash and burn like so many others who have tried to cross over to acting from another profession. Johnson's first movies were exactly what you would have expected: a big muscle-bound man walking around intimidating everyone around him and botching the limited dialogue that was given to him. (Duane, if you are reading this, please keep reading before threatening me with the "people's elbow" because I'm about to brag about you.) The movie posters read, "co-starring The Rock." He had some commercial success, much like the dancer mentioned in the intro, because he brought with him the skills of live performance and bodybuilding. As an actor, however, he wasn't very good, and these same bankable attributes that got him started would end up being his biggest obstacles. He didn't want to be known as The Rock anymore. He had a name. He was an actor. But if you weren't a fan of WWF wrestling, I doubt you were lining up to watch his movies. As an acting coach, I wasn't an early fan, either, but I couldn't help noticing this guy wasn't going away. His movie appearances became more frequent. Although still not what I would consider to be great acting, his performances kept getting markedly better each year. I remember saying to my wife, "You know, I just watched a movie that had The Rock in it. You'd be surprised. This guy is starting to get really good."

Now, almost 20 years after his famous WWF wrestling days, The Rock is a distant memory, and Duane Johnson has become a household name. He is a leading man with the acting chops to match his striking look. He has taken on roles in romantic comedies and voiced one of Disney's biggest hit characters, Maui, in the movie *Moana*. So keep this story in mind as you lay down your foundation and begin the wonderful journey into acting. Duane Johnson was already famous and had mastery-level skills when it came to his body and live performance. Since leaving his old fame behind, it still took him twenty years and 103 credits to earn the talent he has today. And there's no doubt in my mind that Mr. Johnson is still beating the pavement each and every day because that's what it takes.

"Be humble. Be hungry. And always be the hardest worker in the room. Success isn't always about greatness. It's all about consistency. Consistent hard work gains success. Greatness will come." —Duane Johnson

There is no finish line, friends. Become a student for life, and I guarantee success will come knocking on your door!

CREATE GOOD HABITS

I understand this isn't a new concept, but I couldn't write a book about making money without including a section on habits. You are reading this book because you want to be successful. I wrote this book because I'm passionate about helping others become successful. Habit creation is, for most of us, head knowledge, but not a living, breathing truth. We know we should go to bed at a certain time, exercise five days a week, pray or meditate, and do the work required to live a meaningful existence. Yet I hear so many students tell me that sticking to a new habit feels impossible. Well, it's not. If you can't stick to a decision to become better every single day no matter what, I suggest you go back to your "why" because it's not strong enough. (For more on this refer to Chapter 6—Run the Business.)

In author Annie Dillard's words, "How we spend our days is, of course, how we spend our lives." You will become an average of the things you do, the thoughts that consume your mind, and the people you surround yourself with on a daily basis. So don't dismiss working on your habits as common knowledge. This is quite possibly the most important section of this entire book. Good habits will ensure forward progress, and forward progress over time is the only thing that matters.

There are many great books written on self development and almost all of them include a section on habit formation. This is not on accident. I recommend reading as many of these as you can get your hands on. (A list of recommended books on this subject can be found at www.DearingStudio.com/ActingIsMyDayJob). I can tell you from first-hand experience that you cannot get rid of a bad habit without first replacing it with a good one. So rather than trying to cut things out of your life, start by infusing new patterns that will leave you feeling good and are in line with achieving your long-term goals. As these new patterns set in, you'll quickly find that there will be less room for the old ways of doing things. Never drop a habit without replacing it with a new one. For example, my life changed completely when I decided one day that to be a top acting and business coach, I would begin habitually waking up at 4am to exercise, read, and write. I knew that this daily habit, if followed rigorously, would be the critical ingredient to my success. I anchored myself with a strong "why" and never looked back. Soon I found myself accomplishing more on one day before 8AM than I used to in an entire week. This habit provided a whole new energy and enthusiasm for my craft. This quickly led to a change in diet, exercise, and many other positive shifts. That one added habit snowballed into everything I do.

You, too, have something inside that you know you should be doing. Don't wait. Within a few years, you truly won't recognize yourself. Yes, this is hard work. It may take a few tries to train your body and mind to follow suit with your new goals and challenges, but it will be worth it if you stick with it. Your body and mind will praise you.

Please understand: these goals were specific to me, my mind, my body, my spirit, and my life. You must create *your own* custom set of habits to carve out the specific career of your dreams. Also notice that the snowball didn't start with me trying to "stop sleeping in." Remember to add a good habit, and the bad ones will melt away on their own. I'm going to end this section by laying out a list of good habits every serious actor should adapt into their lives. Here are the essentials:

Read

A portion of every day should be spent reading. There aren't enough hours in a lifetime to read all the wonderful books on acting, award-winning plays, and wonderful screenplays. So just make it a habit to read something acting related for at least 20 minutes every day. (A list of recommended acting books, scripts and plays can be found at www.DearingStudio.com/ActingIsMyDayJob).

Write

As an artist, it is important to understand the beauty and power of the written word. Creating a habit to write every day will provide the actor deeper access to language, and birth a new respect for those who write the scripts you dream to have the privilege to act out. It will force you to ask better questions when you analyze someone else's writing. "Why did she choose this word?" "What is the music of this writing?" Your daily writing could be as simple as a journal. Alternatively, it could be a monologue for a character you're working on, or a much larger creative endeavor to be produced. Just put pen to paper (or fingers to keys) every day.

Speak

A writer's job is to write the words. An actor's job is to bring those words to life. The actor must be constantly working on ways to improve their sound when speaking. Every day should include some time dedicated to beautiful, precise speech. This means you need to address your diction, posture, and vocal stamina for getting through long pieces of dialogue. Practice this on a daily basis in your everyday activities. Use what you learn as you chat with friends and family, or even to yourself. You must change the way you speak in life to change the way you speak on stage. Even something as simple as breathing properly will become a revelation when you learn to do it well. (As master acting coach Larry Moss loves to say, "Breath is preparation for the idea.") Finally, a few singing lessons are also a worthy investment for any actor to consider. The basic exercises learned in a vocal lesson will open up your speaking instrument.

Memorize

Memorization is a part of the job. You'll need to work on this for the rest of your career. It's not the most glamorous part of your job. No excuses; just do it. You likely won't feel like doing this every day. You're going to want to claim that memorization is "too hard" or "not one of your strengths." Get over it. Memorization is a skill that can be improved upon, like anything else, through diligent practice and repetition. Do some research on various techniques to find what works for you. Whether you memorize better with the help of a recorder, repetition, or chunking out blocks of text, you can find a strategy that works for you. No matter the technique you choose, be sure to separate the memorization from the performance. (For more on "how to memorize," visit our acting school blog www.DearingStudio.com/blog for a full breakdown on the process).

Exercise

Actors are musicians without an instrument. We have ourselves, our ideas, our emotional life, and our creative fire; that's the music we play. It is imperative that you keep yourself physically fit and ready to take on whatever challenge may come, and understand that your body is the instrument. Actors come in every shape and size, so don't think you need to be thin or buff to be successful. Rather, you need to be *the best version of yourself* at any given moment. Daily exercise will keep you strong and provide an internal confidence that is needed to be successful.

Overcome

Most people either never begin acting, or they quit within the first couple years, because of fear. I suggest, rather than being scared and waiting until something comes after you, go out and seek to overcome your fear. Look for some obstacle to overcome every day. Are you afraid to be in front of the camera? Then set up the camera today and hit record. Are you afraid of

Shakespeare? Download a monologue and begin to memorize it. Once you face a fear, it tends to go away, and a new fear will emerge. As you progress in acting, the stages become bigger and the pressure will build. You can't eliminate fear, but you can get good at facing it head on.

Play

Actors must be free. This is the easiest thing to say, and maybe the single hardest thing to do. Children are so delightful to watch as they go about their business of playing. They impersonate, imitate, move, and create with utter abandon. They haven't learned to be self-aware yet. As adults, we have to re-learn this skill, and it's not easy. Get into an improv group or something similar. Find ways to be silly with your kids and friends. The idea is to lose your self-consciousness as often as possible. To be a great actor, you must be willing to be yourself, and to feel real feelings, all while being watched. This takes practice, and intentional playtime will help.

PURSUE MASTERY

To pursue mastery is to let go of the end result and focus instead on the process. I hope by reading this book, I have convinced you that being a successful actor, though not easy, is possible. It's been said that it takes ten thousand hours to master a particular skill. Actors have so many skills that feed one another that in this craft there will never be an end to your learning process.

The good news is that once you set your aim on developing skill rather than obsessing over opportunities you can't control, you'll start to harvest success. Along the pathway to mastery, there are many gifts that will come your way. You'll be surprised how easy it will be to land an agent once you have released "getting an agent" from your goal sheet. Remember to set your sights on getting better every day, and you will systematically increase your value. You'll become so good, the industry will have no choice but to hire you.

Perhaps the most difficult aspect of becoming an actor is dealing with the unknown. There's no ending point where someone will hand you a degree. Initially, you won't be guaranteed a job that pays a certain amount per year. But this challenge is also what makes being an actor so great: the ceiling for what you can do doesn't exist. Your potential is limitless. I've seen people walk into our studio completely raw, work incredibly hard, and become the next Disney star. I've seen others use these skills to get a promotion at work or overcome a speech impediment. Acting is an artform that has the power to make you a better person as you seek to find your path as a performer.

I've also seen many people with pretty faces and a bit of "start-up talent" who squandered away potential careers because they lacked the work ethic and determination to follow through. The difference between those who "make it" and those that don't always comes back to who wants it more. Are you willing to work hard to make your dreams come true? Will you stick it out when times are tough and it seems like nothing is going your way? If your focus is on mastery and process instead of getting the gigs, staying the course will be something within your control.

I'll leave you with this story. There was a student of mine who had been training with us for a few years, and he was an exceptional specimen in that he put in 10x the effort of his classmates. Eventually I left a note on his monthly evaluation encouraging him to head to LA. My only condition was that he maintain his work ethic and never quit. I'll never forget the unexpected phone call several years later when this student reached out to tell me he had been cast as the lead in a major network show. He was calling to thank me because the grind had been getting to him and he was on the brink of quitting. He was literally throwing away scripts when he stumbled across my note and remembered the commitment he made not to give up. It was two weeks after finding that note that he auditioned for the role that put him on the map. This actor is now experiencing success beyond his wildest dreams, and he almost let it all go.

You never know when the opportunity will arise to showcase your talent to the world. So it's up to you to prepare each day as if the chance to shine is already within your grasp. To be a champion, you must first think like a champion and train like a champion. You must be willing to do the work when no one is looking. Don't let other people tell you what you can and cannot do. Listen to your heart. If you are supposed to be a great actor, commit to this craft with everything you've got, and don't put it down for anything. By reading this book and implementing the strategies within you have officially become a valued member of the Dearing Acting Studio family. We are here to help so reach out with any questions you may have. I personally cannot wait to hear all about *your story* of success!

*"Matt Dearing changed how I look at acting,
and, in turn, changed my life."*
—*Frank Caliendo, comedian*

Matthew Dearing lives and teaches from the principles of passion, love, and mastery. A professional development coach to elite actors, directors, executives, and corporations, he is the founder of Dearing Acting Studio, Phoenix Casting, and Chaos Comedy Improv. Through speaking engagements, consultations, seminars, and workshops, Matthew has inspired thousands of performers across the globe—many of whom are seen regularly in theaters and on major networks.

In life, always choose to *"act"* with **PASSION**.

At the center of *everything we do* should be **LOVE**.

Happiness comes from a *never-ending pursuit* of **MASTERY**.

*"Thank you Matt for being there to give me guidance and opening my eyes
to how much more I can learn to be a better actress."*
—*Sofia Wylie, High School Musical: The Musical*

Made in the USA
Lexington, KY
06 November 2019

56654553R00059